The Honey Cookbook
Recipes
for Healthy Living

Maria Lo Pinto

HIPPOCRENE BOOKS
New York

Hippocrene paperback edition, 1993.

For information, address:
HIPPOCRENE BOOKS, INC.
171 Madison Avenue
New York, NY 10016
ISBN 0-7818-0149-4

Printed in the United States of America.

Acknowledgments

AMERICAN HONEY INSTITUTE
Harriet M. Grace, *Director*

AUSTRALIAN HONEY INSTITUTE

STATE OF FLORIDA DEPARTMENT OF AGRICULTURE

GEORGIA DEPARTMENT OF ENTOMOLOGY
University of Georgia

HONEY AS A FOOD
E. R. Root

KELLOGG COMPANY

THE SACRED BEE
Hilda M. Ransome

U. S. DEPARTMENT OF AGRICULTURE

ANDRE PROST
Honey Importer of New York City

* * * *

I am especially grateful also to my nieces, Gloria,
Sandra, Mona, Vicky, Geraldine and Angela, and my
nephews Gerald, Jimmy and Tommy for their coopera-
tion and patience. To all my friends who encouraged
me to do this book, especially Helen and Jean, a warm
"thank you."

Contents

Chapter I

Introduction

AS A CHILD, I had been stung by a bee. The memory of the pain lingered for many years, while the bees' service to humanity did not concern me until my recent visit to Sicily.

One bright, balmy summer morning a friend took me on a tour of the hill country nestled in the mountains of Sicily. Our gaily decorated Sicilian donkey cart wound its way through narrow winding roads along the blue Mediterranean Sea, up and down cliffs to the peak of a hill overlooking the Sea. It embraced a picturesque, sleepy little village whose beauty and charm overwhelmed me. Is it real or a painting? I asked.

We dismounted a few feet from a fence covered by giant cacti plants, heavily laden with prickly pears, ripe and sweet, begging to be picked for festive eating. Within this fence stood a small Moorish type house. Its walls were about 15 inches thick and its unusually small casement windows gave the appearance of a miniature fortress.

The orange and lemon trees in the groves about us were in full bloom, exuding their intoxicating perfume. Suddenly, I caught sight of dozens of white bee hives and I instinctively recoiled with horror.

My fears were gradually allayed by the confidence and conviction of my good friend. He led me to the hives and explained the harmlessness and usefulness of bees.

The hustling activity in the hives fascinated me. The bees were engaged in the business of producing honey, for it is a business and a lucrative business indeed. They buzzed in and out of their hives, they vanished into thin air to take nourishment from nearby blossoms or to pollinate plants, that is, to fertilize plants and, loaded with nectar, returned to store it up in their hives. Thus my interest in these dreaded insects and their product was born.

My friend related how he had learned to cultivate and like these industrious little insects. They, in turn, rewarded him with the fruits of their labor by producing vat after vat of golden honey. How did his knowledge benefit humanity besides filling the family coffers?

His father, a physician of repute, was afflicted with the pains and discomfort of ulcers and arthritis. When all remedies failed, he became resigned to his daily diet of milk and honey. To his astonishment this diet evolved into a cure, and, indeed, it was his faith in God and His gifts of nature that produced this cure.

He thus became dedicated to relieving the ills of the people in his neighboring towns and hill villages, and was loved by all who knew him. These towns and villages were bursting with peoples of Greek and Phoenician tradition of which honey was a part. The doctor experimented with honey in the treatment of certain external and internal ailments with phenomenal success, I was told.

Like the father of medicine, Hippocrates, he prescribed for his patients "doses" of honey in combination with other ingredients, and to his patients he became a miracle man. Among his patients was a young girl, suffering from a lung condition, pronounced incurable by other doctors. It was claimed that this good doctor brought her back to a healthy, happy life 8 months after treatments began. He fed her honey with goat's milk, home-made bread, local grown fruits and vegetables, Marsala (sherry) egg nogs and prescribed plenty of rest. I listened wide-eyed to this and many other similar stories. It was this type of experiment and successes that inspired my friend to do further research on the benefits derived from honey, and led to the ultimate venture into the business of producing honey.

Still under the spell of my experience in those little hills, immediately upon my arrival home in New York in 1950, I set upon my adventure of exploring the realms of honey, the bee and its effects upon human beings.

What better subjects could I have chosen than my own family, a group numbering 40 closely-knit persons, with different tastes and preferences in the matter of eating? They ranged from age ten and up: teenagers with facial blemishes common among children in their teens, those with a sweet tooth, one suffering from arthritis, one with stomach acidity, chronic colds, insomnia and other slight disorders that besiege the human being at the most inconvenient times.

I fed them honey in all sorts of dishes and beverages. I made up unguents and masks of honey for their complexions. At first their responses were mixed, as one might imagine, with fear and curiosity, but as time went on their fears were allayed when they found out that I wasn't out to kill them. However, at this point I can only say with glee that many of the conditions complained of were substantially relieved, with the result that I was encouraged to write this book.

The reaction of my friends, when they were told that this book was being written, was a source of great happiness to me. They immediately embarked on a treasure hunt; some dug down into their recipe files, some into the recesses of their culinary achievements in the distant past; others contributed grandmothers' tales on the folklore of honeys.

Those of us who think of honey only in terms of bread and honey served to our children after school, have a surprise in store. Many are the foods and beverages prepared with honey that are delicate and delightful. The flavor of the honey we use is a matter of preference, of course. As for myself, I like mild blossom honeys. I use them in place of butter and spreads in many ways. Moreover, I find them more economical in the long run, less fattening and more digestible.

Research has indicated that honey neutralizes acids in foods and in one's stomach. It assimilates rapidly and easily and is non-irritating to the delicate membrane of the digestive system. It is known to curb our craving for too sweet desserts after meals and the desire for the very spicy foods many of us cannot afford to indulge in. There are few of us who are not familiar with the important part that honey plays in the fields of medicine and cosmetics.

The art of cooking, for most people all over the world, is a delightful, sacred or therapeutic adventure. Most Europeans and Orientals prepare their meals with a great deal of loving care and patience. Good cooking and proper feeding are important factors in the general well-being and happiness of the family. These elements in homemaking have been neglected in this generation, however, because many women work outside the home, either to secure luxuries or to avoid boredom. They have still to learn that a homemaker can become as artistic and creative in her own kitchen as in any other outside activity she may undertake to dispense with the tensions and neuroses so common in modern American life. Well-prepared recipes are truly conversation pieces and always arouse interest.

Whether or not the incentive to this creative challenge includes honey in cooking, it is my firm belief that a more wholesome attitude toward culinary experiences carries its own reward. It is truly amazing that today so many survive badly prepared meals and have never been able to appreciate the stimulus of well-prepared, eye-appealing food because taste buds are discouraged by haste in preparation.

Therefore, my friends, it is my hope that you will find herein interesting and useful material which will lead to new experiences in your kitchen and to new heights of happiness, beauty and health.

MARIA LO PINTO

CHAPTER II

Legend and Superstition

EGYPT was described in the Bible as the land of milk and honey. The fertility of its land was attributed to the existence of its numerous bees.

The properties and value of honey were praised in song and story before the written word was known to the ancient world. The psalms of David were among the first poetic tributes to honey, the honeycomb and the industrious little bee.

The legends of ancient Greece refer to the honey distilled by the bees, the chemists of their day, as "Dew distilled from the stars and the rainbow, trickling down by way of the flowers, into the mouths of new-born babes and into the food of men." It was the nectar and ambrosia of the immortal Greek gods and mortal children. To the ancient Greeks, it served the same purpose that wine did after its discovery centuries later.

Homer, the blind Greek poet, tells that when Hekamede celebrated the heroism of Nestor and Machaon, she set before them a vessel of bronze containing onions for relish, pale honey and the grain of sacred barley.

Democritus, a Greek philosopher, known as the laughing philosopher and honey-lover, believed that the very aroma of honey prolonged life. In the Greek legend, he decided at the age of 109 to hasten his death by giving up the use of honey. However, his family, eager to celebrate a special festival, urged him to survive the feast. He agreed and ordered that a jar of honey be brought to him at frequent intervals. Inhaling its aroma kept him alive during the feast. After the feast he refused the honey and died. But, before his death, he requested that his body be annointed with honey so that he might make up for the lack during his life-time.

In ancient Athens, offerings of a dish of honey, three white almonds, a loaf of bread and a glass of water, were made to the gods when imploring aid.

We are told that Spartan women made long, weary journeys to place a honey cake in a certain cave, where the Fates were ever-present though invisible, to gain their favor. On the third or fifth night after the birth of a child, the house door was left open or unlatched and a table set with many honeyed dainties for the Fates to partake and confer their many blessings on the new-born babe.

And Roman legend imparts to us the knowledge that stalwart Romans usually owned hives. Their food and beverages nearly always contained honey. As a gesture of hospitality they generally offered their guests honey from their own hives.

The Roman warriors, it is said, took their bee hives with them when launching an attack on the enemy because the bee was feared as a deadly weapon.

When the poet Virgil's farm was confiscated by the army, his faithful servants set the family treasures in a ring of hives, and scared away the brave soldiers of the Roman Legions by stirring up the bees. These soldiers were not phased by spears, swords and even wild elephants, but they fled in panic from the tiny, piercing daggers of the angry bees.

Honey was so valuable to the Romans that it was used as payment for taxes. It was also donated by citizens of certain Roman towns to priests because they required large quantities of honey for their religious rites.

In Finland a bride's mouth was smeared with honey to keep her faithful. There is an old Dutch law that honey placed on the lips of an unwanted child makes it illegal for a father to ignore him and obligatory to make the child an equal heir.

Among the Italians, there is the following saying: "Madame,

treat your husband with honey and you will possess his heart. Sir, treat your wife as you did during your honey-moon and peace shall always reign supreme in your home."

In the Orient honey played an important part in the birth, marriage and burial rites of the Brahman Indians.

For instance, when a child was born, his mouth was touched with a golden spoon or a piece of gold. Then, during the rite, the child was fed with honey and butter as the father proclaimed: "I give thee this honey food so that the gods may protect thee and that thou mayst live a hundred autumns in this world."

The Hindus gave honey and curd to the bridegroom when he came to the bride's house. Honey was sometimes offered at a marriage ceremony. When the groom kissed the bride he used to say, "Honey, this is honey, the speech of thy tongue is honey, in my mouth lives the honey of the bee, in my teeth lives peace."

In ancient India, as in Greece and Rome, there were many superstitions connected with bees. Swarming was observed carefully. A swarm entering a house denoted misfortune.

To dream of bees resting on a building was interpreted to mean that evil would befall the building and the dreamer would suffer some great misfortune or even lose his life.

The people of India also believed that putting a few drops of honey in the eyes would cure cataracts, and even today there are those who have tried it and believe it to be true.

Honey and the honey comb are referred to many times in the Holy Bible. In the Talmud it is stated that honey is a remedy for various diseases, such as those known today as gout and heart trouble. It also suggests honey for healing the wounds of man and beast and recommends that it be mixed with wine.

We are told that the ancient Hebrews were forbidden to offer sacrifices of honey because it was subject to fermentation under certain conditions. However, it was permitted as a "not-burnt" offering of the first fruits of the season. They believed that honey made people witty and intelligent. The prophets ordered eating of honey because it was a delicious and healing food bringing good luck to the consumer. And, we observe that Hebrew festivals to this day include the use of honey, unadorned and in cakes and desserts.

Chapter III

The Honey Bee

AMONG the family of insects which store up the nectar of flowers for food, is the honey bee. The industry of this little insect, pollinating the flowers, producing honey and honey wax and forming highly organized colonies, gives rise to such human attributes as being "as busy as a bee," "thrifty as a bee."

"And still they gazed and still the wonder grew" that so inconspicuous a little insect could be of so much service to man. By its pollination, it has become a great agricultural factor and a boon to the production of fruits and many vegetables. Without the activity of the bee many plants would neither seed nor produce fruit. Its product can be a source of health and beauty and pleasure to humanity.

The well organized colony constitutes three types of bees: the drone (the lazy bee) which mates with the queen; the queen bee which lays the eggs and supervises; and the worker that builds the hives and cares for the colony in the bee hive. It is the worker that gathers the nectar or pollen from the flowers to store in the hive.

The keeper of the bees held an important place in ancient Egypt as well as in Greece, for honey was of great significance in the life and religion of the old world. In Greece the keepers of bees used to move their hives to all parts of the country, following the seasons, crops and flowers.

Bees were used as symbols on coins, on walls and as decorative motifs among the aristocracy of Greece, Egypt and ancient Rome, and even in modern France.

BEESWAX

The Egyptians used beeswax for preserving mummies. It was used to seal coffins in order to make them airtight; to preserve the body, wax was rubbed over the corpse.

Beeswax was also used by sorcerers of Babylon, India, Greece and Rome to make figures of men and animals, to conjure up evil spirits. The ancients believed that if a figure of a man, made by a witch, was injured or destroyed, it was an omen of suffering or death to the man.

Beeswax was used to make church candles. The wax candles were considered as a symbol of the Saviour by the church of Rome at its inception. The candle denoted the body of Christ because it comprised the wax from the best and sweetest smelling flowers used by the bees. The wick symbolized the soul and mortality of Christ; the light, the divine spirit.

Waxen images served as offerings of thanksgiving for some favor hoped for or received from above. This custom prevails to this day. The Italians of southern Italy, on certain feast days, carry lighted candles and tapers in processions following the image of their patron saint who has bestowed some special favor on the follower.

Wax figures were also symbolic to the Germanic people. In childless homes, waxen figures were offered to the church in the hope that it would bring about the birth of a child to the married couple.

Along with honey, the beeswax had many important uses, yes, even to the extent that it was used as a dowry and the payment of taxes.

In modern times in addition to candle making, it is an important ingredient in floor waxes, polishes, shoe polishes, and in many cosmetics, such as face creams and lipsticks.

18

KINDS OF HONEY

Honey, as we have seen, is the nectar of flowers, collected, modified and stored by the honey bee in small waxen cells of the honeycomb. The aromatic substances on which the bee feeds give the honey its characteristic flavor and color. Since the bee gathers the nectar from various flowers, blossoms, herbs and shrubs in many parts of the world, the honey varies accordingly in color and flavor.

There are mild honeys and there are tangy, spicy honeys. There is honey in liquid form and there is crystalized or granulated honey.

Some honeys are almost white, like water, colorless; some honeys are light amber; some dark amber. Usually, the lighter the color, the milder the flavor; the darker, the stronger and spicier the flavor.

Sweet clover, white clover and alfalfa are the main sources of the milder honeys in the United States. Buckwheat is the source of the stronger flavored honey.

Distinctly flavored honeys come from the tupelo tree of the south, from orange, lemon and cotton blossoms, from wild sage, avocado, mountain lilac and eucalyptus from California and the southwest, wild thyme and many others from other parts of the country and from all over the world.

From Greece comes the famous Mt. Hymetus honey, praised by the Greek gods and men. It is very popular among gourmets for its distinctive flavor, and comes from wild thyme. It is noted for its special slightly tangy perfume-flavor.

From Sicily come the very delicate, very light amber-colored orange and lemon blossom honeys.

Australia gives us eucalyptus honey which very often is in crystalized form, making it easier to spread without running over.

Trappist honey from Canada is produced by the Trappist monks; heather honey comes from Scotland, Narbonne honey from France, and many other delicate honeys from other parts of the world.

Since people in the United States are becoming more honey-minded and are beginning to realize the virtues and the many advantages in the use of honey, more and more honeys are being brought into this country from Europe, Asia, Africa and South America.

Honey is marketed in several forms: Extracted or liquid honey, section comb, comb honey, bulk comb and creamed.

The liquid honey is the most popular. It is strained and filtered, packed in glass jars and in cans.

Section comb is taken from the beehive, cut into sections and placed in small wooden frames. Some like to eat it as a confection right out of the frame.

Bulk comb, also called chunk honey, consists of pieces of honeycomb with extracted honey poured over it. This too is sold in glass jars or cans.

Creamed honey is made from granulated or crystalized honey, run through a food grinder once or twice and whipped with a paddle or beater. Sometimes, liquid honey is beaten into the granulated honey to make a smoother spread.

CHAPTER IV

Stars in Your Eyes

ARISTOXEMUS (320 B.C.) claimed that anyone who ate honey, spring onions and bread for his daily breakfast, would be free from all diseases throughout his lifetime. This may sound like an unusual, off the beaten path, breakfast but one that might be worth trying.

Hippocrates, the father of medicine, prescribed honey for those who wished to live long, happy lives. In fact, some southern Italians still believe that if one drinks wine sweetened with honey and eats bread daily, one's life is bound to be long and healthy.

My own experiences, mentioned in the introduction to this book, and the legends and beliefs of the ancient world with respect to the goodness of honey have further encouraged me to write this volume. Moreover, there is a growing tendency on the part of many modern doctors to recognize its value in everyday use, in foods, cosmetics and medicine.

As mentioned earlier, I have used honey in cooking, baking and as a substitute for sugar and syrups. I have prepared simple formulae for minor skin and throat irritations with success, and I have used honey for simple digestive discomfort with gratifying results. And, of course, its been such fun!

The following 'recipes' are not offered by a professional in the field of cosmetics and medicine, or a self-styled practitioner of medicine. These are simple homeopathic remedies that can do no harm, but will benefit the average normally healthy person, will enhance beauty, improve health and provide great sat-

21

isfaction from "doing it yourself" at little expense. This will put "stars in your eyes."

HONEY FOR HEALTH

DID YOU KNOW THAT:

Daily use of honey creates heat, energy, wards off fatigue and aids recuperative powers.

Because it has been found that honey has a dietetic value by inducing the free flow of saliva, its daily use aids digestion and is invaluable to weak and squeamish stomachs.

Furthermore, honey is not only a valuable food, and a popular medicine, it is an important component of liniments and plasters with magic healing powers.

In some Swiss sanitoriums, high up in the Alps, patients suffering from anemia and other ailments are, according to clinical experiments, restored to health with the addition of honey and goat's milk to their diets.

And in Europe, where doctors are subsidized by the government, they prescribe honey frequently to keep people healthy. Many surgeons of the old world used honey for dressing wounds to expedite healing, and I know several modern doctors who use prescriptions containing large portions of honey for that purpose.

Even veterinarians and farmers use honeyed mashes to produce better cattle and poultry.

Today we are all more or less conscious of the fact that health and beauty go hand in hand, so here are a few "formulae" that will help you see the world through rose-colored glasses:

FOR MILD SORE THROAT:

    1 cup boiling water
    4 sage leave, fresh, or ¼ tsp. sage powder

Combine and steep 10 minutes; strain; add 1 tablespoon honey and 1 tablespoon cider vinegar. Mix well. Use lukewarm as a gargle several times a day.

2 tbs. buckwheat honey	2 tbs. lemon juice
2 tsp. glycerin	⅛ tsp. powdered ginger

Combine and heat in a jar, over hot water. When well blended, shake jar vigorously. Sip a teaspoonful slowly at night before going to bed. It will soothe your throat. Use warm or at room temperature.

FOR INSOMNIA:

The hypnotic power of honey is often referred to in Greek and Roman mythology. According to Orpheus, the god of sleep, if anyone falls asleep after eating honey it is difficult to awake him.

If we sleep well, we are refreshed the next morning. We make life pleasant for everyone around us and we are able to cope with our daily problems whatever they may be.

Too many sleeping pills can be dangerous. Here are a few simple remedies to help you sleep better:

1. Scald 1 cup of milk, sweetened with 1 tablespoon honey. If you wish, add 1 teaspoon rum or sherry. Drink while hot before bedtime. Repeat 3 or 4 nights in succession and you will be surprised how it will relax you and what a nice comfortable feeling you will have the next morning. If goat's milk is to your liking and it is available, so much the better.

2. Combine 1 cup of hot water or weak tea with 1 tablespoon honey and a few fresh or dry mint leaves; steep 5 minutes; add a clove if you like. Drink before going to bed. You'll sleep like a baby.

FOR ANNOYING COUGHS DUE TO COLDS:

1. Blend well, half cup of your favorite honey with ½ cup

of fresh lemon juice. Pour into jar, cover tightly and shake vigorously. Take teaspoonful as frequently as needed.

2. Dilute 1 tablespoon honey in 1 cup of hot milk or hot water; stir in ¼ teaspoon fresh sweet butter and 1 teaspoonful of good brandy. Blend thoroughly and sip slowly while hot. More effective at bedtime.

3. Blend well ¼ cup of spicy honey with 1 tablespoon fresh lime or lemon juice and 1 tablespoon of pure glycerin, purchased at the drugstore. Keep in covered jar and take 1 teaspoon every two hours or when needed.

4. Cook 1 cup of minced onion with ½ cup of sweet oil in a covered saucepan over moderate heat until onion is soft and mushy (about 20 minutes). Strain in jar. Blend in ½ cup of eucalyptus honey until smooth. Cover jar. Keep at room temperature. Take 1 teaspoon before retiring or when cough bothers you. It soothes the throat.

ASTHMA AND HAY FEVER:

The mountainous areas of Cuba are a haven for bees gathering nectar from rare tropical flowers. This nectar transformed into fine "wonder" honey was used by natives and physicians for many years, for the sick and wounded. This honey was introduced to the United States several years ago and has been subjected to analysis by recognized laboratories (Medical Research Department, Lansing, Michigan) and used in the following ways by physicians and laymen with satisfactory results in many cases.

1. As a food to supplement the diet of sufferers from *digestive disorders.*

2. As a *nasal spray* when diluted with four parts lukewarm, boiled or distilled water, applied two or more times a day.

3. For *hay fever*, the following dosage is prescribed: one or two level teaspoonfuls one-half hour before meals and before retiring.

4. For *Bronchial or Cardiac Asthma.* During an attack, two

teaspoonfuls are taken every twenty minutes for the first hour; one teaspoonful the second hour, and thereafter one teaspoonful every two hours until relieved.

Similar tests have been made with American honeys of all types; these have produced equally effective results.

TONICS

YOUNGSTERS FROM 6 TO 80!

If you feel sluggish and you need a tonic try your hand at these:

Spring or Winter Tonic to enrich your blood and help you get rid of that sluggish feeling:

. . . HONEY-EGG TONIC . . .

3 tbs. mild honey	1 egg yolk
2 tbs. sweet butter, softened	Dash of Salt

Combine and beat all ingredients until smooth and creamy. Store in jar, tightly covered, in refrigerator or cold place.

Spread 1 tablespoon on thin hot toast or hot biscuit; eat about 15 minutes before breakfast and supper. Repeat daily for several weeks or until you feel better. Helps also to maintain normal weight because you are not tempted to overeat at mealtime or eat too many sweet desserts.

For tangy flavor add ½ teaspoon of grated orange rind. Makes a delicious spread for pancakes and waffles too. Especially good for growing children.

. . . SPRING TONIC . . .

To help clear your skin and add sparkle to your eyes:
In a jar, blend 1 cup of honey with 1 teaspoon sulphur powder, purchased at your drug store. Take 1 teaspoon before break-

fast for 21 days at the beginning of the spring season. Good for teenagers.

WATCHING YOUR WEIGHT?

If you are always rushed, jittery and, at the same time, diet conscious, try these:

ONE-GLASS MEAL:

1 cup whole or skimmed milk or dry milk diluted according to instructions on box	1 tbs. mild honey Dash of cinnamon or nutmeg, if desired
1 small egg	1 tbs. sherry, sweet or dry

Beat with rotary beater, all liquids and the egg. Pour in a tall glass and top with cinnamon or nutmeg. Drink cold or at room temperature as desired. This is pleasant tasting, gives energy and nourishment without adding weight.

FOR THE JITTERS:

¾ cup mild honey
3 cups unsweetened grape juice

Blend well and take ½ cup every morning before breakfast or before meals. This will curb your desire for rich fattening foods. Contains many minerals and all the goodness of the fruit.

FOR THAT DEPRESSED FEELING:

. . . SHERRY DELIGHT . . .

This will give you a nice warm glow especially on a cold winter night.

1 pint dry sherry	2 inch cinnamon stick
1 pint water (2 cups)	3 cloves

3 tbs. honey

Combine all ingredients except honey in a saucepan; bring to a slow boil. Cover. Boil slowly for 10 minutes. Add honey and stir. Remove from fire. Strain and serve hot in cups or glasses.

FOR THAT GRIPPY FEELING:

1 cup red tart wine, hot   1 tbs. lemon juice
2 tbs. mild honey

Combine and stir until well blended. Drink slowly before going to bed. Repeat twice daily until you feel better. Stay indoors and rest if possible.

FOR MILD CHEST COLD: (If condition persists call your doctor)

1 tbs. of buckwheat honey or   1 cup of hot milk
    a mild flavored honey   1 tsp. sweet butter

Blend well and sip slowly before bedtime, and, any time, until you feel better.

TO LIFT YOUR SPIRITS AND SWEETEN YOUR BREATH:

. . . ROSEMARY-MINT TEA . . .

1 quart boiling water
25 fresh rosemary leaves or 1 tsp. dry leaves
25 fresh mint leaves or 1 tbs. dry leaves
3 tbs. honey of desired flavor (orange blossom honey
    is recommended here)

Combine in quart jar; steep for 24 hours in cool place. Strain. Drink half cup before bedtime, either cold or lukewarm, when you have a sour stomach or bad breath from over-indulgence.

HONEY IN COSMETICS

According to the ancient orientals, if a bee stings you, pat the sting with honey. In taking the advice of the orientals your author has been spared many uncomfortable hours of pain and swelling as the result of bee stings.

Boils, sore pimples and superficial burns also heal faster when covered with a bit of pure honey. Burns may be treated by applying honey every four hours. Repeat until condition clears.

In case of serious burns see your doctor.

FOR SKIN SCRAPES AND MILD SURFACE SKIN IRRITATIONS:
(Not due to allergies)

Combine equal parts honey and vinegar. Blend well and pat affected parts with sterilized cotton, soaked in solution. Repeat every 4 hours until condition clears. If used before going to bed cover lightly with gauze.

Make sure skin is clean before applying.

If condition persists see your doctor.

MAKING YOUR OWN TOILET PREPARATIONS:

Honey has long been recognized as a true cosmetic. It is an ingredient of many fine creams and lotions today. It is nourishing and refining to the skin and, when combined with other ingredients, it is more effective as a skin beautifier, softener and cleanser.

The ancient volumes written in praise of honey for beauty and health have apparently contributed wisdom and understanding to our modern beauty experts and cosmetic manufacturers. In recent months there has been a great deal of publicity about an expensive face cream known as "Royal Jelly." This cream according to beauty experts is supposed to give that "perpetually youthful appearance" to the user. What do you suppose the main ingredient of this "Royal Jelly" is? Of course, it is a substance produced by the glands of queen bees. It is also known as "bee-milk." A number of French scientists in their extensive experiments with honey and royal jelly have found that both of these products possess miraculous powers of rejuvenation and prolonging life. "Royal" because it is produced primarily by the queen bee.

Do try these. They may be a bit sticky but lukewarm water soon removes any application.

The following formulae are given in small proportions in order that it may be easier for you to prepare them. They are as effective and certainly more economical than many cosmetics.

. . . FACIAL MASKS . . .

Oatmeal Facial

⅓ cup finely ground oatmeal
3 tsp. honey, or enough honey to make a smooth paste

1 tsp. of rose water or orange flower water

Blend oatmeal with honey until well mixed. If too thick and unmanageable add a little rose water or orange flower water. Spread over clean face and leave it on for about ½ hour. Relax while it is on if you can. Remove with soft washcloth and warm water. Rinse with cold water or an astringent. *Substitutes*: Almond meal or corn meal may be used if desired.

This does wonders for your skin. Try it once a week and see the difference. It is especially helpful for oily or normal skins.

Because the ancient Chinese knew that honey had a nourishing, bleaching, astringent and antiseptic effect on the skin, they used it profusely for all kinds of skin disorders. This recipe was a favorite one according to legend.

29

. . . FACE AND HAND CREAM . . .

1 tsp. almond oil	2 tbs. light honey
2 drops of favorite perfume	1 small egg yolk

Combine all ingredients in the order named, in a small bowl. Beat until fluffy. Store in small covered jar in a cold place. Apply on clean face or hands; leave on about 20 minutes; rinse off with lukewarm water; then cold water. Pat dry.

This tones and smooths the skin, helps to prevent wrinkles, heals blemishes and chapped hands.

. . . MADAME DU BARRY'S HONEY FACIAL . . .

Clean your face and neck with your favorite cream. Wipe off. With a piece of cotton pat on some warm witch hazel to open the pores. With finger tips pat on a pure mild honey until your face and neck are covered and begin to tingle. Then lie down for about a half hour and let the honey soak in. Remove with washcloth wrung in warm water. Splash with cold water several times and you will feel like a new gal.

Try this before going on a special date, or once a week to soften and smooth your skin.

TO REFRESH AND REJUVENATE YOUR SKIN:

. . . CLEOPATRA'S HEART BALM . . .

1 teaspoon honey blended with 1 tablespoon milk and the white of a small egg. Beat well and apply to clean face and neck. Leave on about one-half hour or as long as you wish. When it feels dry and brittle wash it off with lukewarm water; rinse with cold water. Apply make up. You will feel the muscles of your neck and face tingle.

No wonder Antony was mad about Cleo. She used this formula on her entire body to keep her skin beautiful and soft.

FOR SKIN DISCOLORATION AND FRECKLES:

6 tbs. lemon or orange blossom honey	1 tbs. alcohol
1 tbs. glycerin	6 ounces essence of ambergris
	1 teaspoon lemon juice

Combine honey and glycerin in a jar. Place jar in saucepan of warm water and bring water to the boiling point. Remove from fire. Cover jar and shake well. When cool add balance of ingredients and blend by shaking the jar some more. Apply to clean face before going to bed, or leave it on while you do your housework. Wash off with lukewarm water and rinse with cold water.

. . . ALMOND HAND CREAM . . .

1 tbs. rose water	2 ½ tbs. almond meal or finely
1 tsp. olive oil	ground almonds, blanched
2 tbs. honey	

Combine the ingredients and blend until smooth and creamy. If too thin gradually add about ½ teaspoon of cornstarch, blend until medium soft cream is obtained.

This bleaches and softens the hands. Rub well into your hands any time when you are not working or before bedtime. Wear loose fitting gloves for protection if you wish. Wash off with warm water, then cold.

. . . HAND MEAL . . .

3 tbs. finely ground corn meal	2 tbs. honey
1 tsp. cornstarch	

Blend well in the order named. Place in small jar. Use as you would any hand soap. Softens, cleans and smooths the hands. Always rinse hands with cold water.

. . . UNGUENTS FOR BURNS . . .

Make a paste of equal parts of honey and baking soda; spread on burn and cover lightly with gauze. Relieves pain and that burning sensation.

If the burn is serious see your doctor.

1 tbs. distilled water or boiled water, cooled	2 tbs. honey
	2 tbs. cornstarch

Blend into a smooth paste and apply to burn. Cover lightly with sterile gauze.

. . . LEG ULCERS, SMALL WOUNDS AND CHILBLAIN . . .

A Chinese doctor, K. L. Yong (*Chinese Medical Journal* 62:55, 1944), has found that honey, which is plentiful in most parts of China, may be used in treating ordinary leg ulcers, small wounds and chilblains. Because honey has a high sugar content it is bacteriostatic; while, owing to its yellow pigment, it might be rich in vitamin A.

A honey ointment was prepared, consisting of one-fifth petroleum jelly or vaseline and four-fifths of the mildest and purest honey available. The application of this ointment on clean wounds or ulcers met with great success in that it gave relief from pain and swelling and healed wounds faster than some other medications.

We are also told that cod liver oil and honey used in the above proportions, makes an ointment of great efficacy for ulcers and wounds. (Red Cross hospital, Hamburg, Germany)

Worried about wrinkles and crow feet? Then try this:

. . . SOOTHING FACE CREAM . . .

1 tbs. melted white bees wax or lanolin	2 tbs. rose water or orange blossom water
3 tbs. honey	½ tsp. olive oil
1 tbs. lemon juice	

Melt half ounce of wax in a glass jar over hot water. When melted leave 1 tablespoon of melted wax in the jar and save the balance of the wax. Add honey and lemon juice and blend well with a teaspoon. Keep jar in pan with hot water while you are mixing the ingredients. Add the oil and blend some more. When mixture is smooth and creamy remove pan from fire and add rose water. Stir well and cover jar. Remove jar from pan. If wax separates from mixture stir with finger to mix well, while still warm.

Apply cream when cool to face and neck that have been washed with soap and warm water and rinsed in cool water. Leave on about half an hour and rinse with warm water then cold. Apply make up if you are going out. Or leave on all night.

FOR CHAFFED SKIN AND MILD SUNBURN:

2 tbs. honey	1 tbs. pure alcohol or toilet water
2 tbs. glycerin	
2 tbs. lemon juice	

Place in a small jar and shake until contents are well mixed. Apply when needed.

FOR CHAPPED LIPS AND SKIN:

Blend in a small jar: 2 tablespoons honey; 2 tablespoons lemon juice; 2 tablespoons of your favorite cologne or toilet water. Pat on frequently with fingertips.

33

CHAPTER V

Cooking with Honey

DIET! Diet! everyone, these days, is diet-conscious and with good reason. We deprive ourselves of this, that and the other food because we fear they are fattening. We literally starve our bodies of much needed energy foods, vitamins and minerals because we worry about that spare tire around our middle. We therefore become listless, we lose the spring in our steps and our pleasant disposition.

Experience has taught me that rigid dieting is detrimental to our health and peace of mind. It makes nervous wrecks out of us.

Everything we eat has some vital food value that helps preserve our bodies and keeps our minds alert. I contend that if we eat normal portions of food (including sweets in moderation), necessary for energy and vigor, if we do not overeat or eat between meals, and take a moderate amount of exercises and fresh air the results will be normal weight, a healthy body and a sunny disposition. Of course, if we are "glandular" that is another matter.

It is my personal experience and probably yours, that when we go on a strict diet we may lose a few pounds temporarily, but as soon as we resume our old eating habits, we regain the lost poundage plus a few extras.

Many people believe that honey is fattening because it is a sweetener. I have found that this is not so. Taken daily in small quantities in any form, especially when dieting, it gives that

35

added zest that we need. It stifles a craving for rich desserts. Honey contains small quantities of minerals, vitamins, hormones and even small amounts of copper and iron so necessary to the normal formation of hemoglobin and is nutritious without adding excessive weight.

Laboratory tests in universities all over the world and tests made by the Department of Agriculture show that honey is about one-fourth water and about three-fourths sugar, chiefly lebulose, known as fruit sugar, and dextrose also known as grape sugar. It is an alkalizer and easy to digest; it is quickly absorbed into the blood stream thus giving quick soothing energy; and it is frequently used in kidney ailments and gallstone conditions.

BREADS AND MUFFINS

. . . ENRICHED BREAD . . .

2 cups milk or 1 cup milk and	2 tbs. honey
1 cup water	1 cake compressed or dry yeast
1 tbs. salt	6 cups enriched flour (about)
2 tbs. shortening	sifted
2 tbs. warm milk	

Scald milk and cool to lukewarm. Add salt and shortening. Put 2 tablespoons of warm milk, honey and yeast in mixing bowl; let stand until yeast is softened. Mix slightly. Add milk mixture and half the flour. Beat thoroughly. Gradually add enough flour to make a soft dough. Turn out on floured board and knead until smooth and elastic. This requires about 8 minutes. Place in slightly greased bowl and let rise until double in bulk. Punch down slightly and let rise again. Form into 2 loaves. Place in greased pans. Allow to rise until double in bulk. Bake about 40 minutes at 400° F. or until bread shrinks from sides of pans.

. . . ELAIN'S OATMEAL BREAD . . .

1 cup oatmeal	2 cups boiling water
2 tsp. salt	1 yeast cake
½ cup dark honey (either buck-	⅓ cup lukewarm water
wheat or a blend)	5 ½ cups (about) all purpose flour
4 tbs. fat	Melted butter

In a large bowl combine first four ingredients with boiling water. Mix well. Let stand until cool.

Dissolve yeast in lukewarm water and let stand about five minutes or according to instructions on wrapper and add to mixture.

Add enough flour to make a medium soft dough that can be kneaded easily and not stick to board. Knead about 8 minutes on lightly floured board. Set aside in large covered bowl in a warm place to rise until double its bulk. Then punch down and divide into two loaves. Knead 5 minutes. Place dough in large greased loaf pans. Brush top with butter, cover with a towel and let rise until double its bulk. Bake at 375° F. for 45 minutes or until bread shrinks from sides of pans. Remove from oven and pans; place on rack to cool. Keeps fresh for days.

. . . ELSA'S DATE NUT BREAD . . .

1 cup boiling water	1 ½ cups enriched flour
1 cup chopped dates	¾ tbs. salt
2 tbs. shortening	2 tsp. baking powder
¾ cup honey	1 cup broken nut meats
1 egg	

Add boiling water to chopped dates and cook about 2 minutes stirring constantly. Melt shortening. Add honey gradually, beating well. Add egg and beat. Add date mixture. Add sifted dry ingredients and nuts. Mix well. Pour mixture into greased loaf pan 4½ x 8½ inches. Bake at 325° F. for 1 hour or until done. Yields: 1 loaf.

. . . HONEY ALL-BRAN ORANGE BREAD . . .

1 egg	1 cup All-Bran
1 ½ tbs. grated orange rind	2 ½ cups sifted flour
¾ cup orange juice	2 ½ tsp. baking powder
1 cup honey	½ tsp. baking soda
2 tbs. soft shortening	½ tsp. salt

Beat together in mixing bowl, egg, orange rind, orange juice, honey and shortening. Add All-Bran and let stand about 10 minutes.

Sift together flour, baking powder, soda and salt. Add to All-Bran mixture, stirring *only until combined*. Spread in greased 9½ x 5¼-inch loaf pan.

Bake in slow oven (325° F.) about 1 hour and 10 minutes. Yield: 1 loaf.

. . . JEAN'S ORANGE NUT BREAD . . .

2 tbs. shortening	2 ¼ cups flour
1 cup honey	⅛ tsp. soda
1 egg, small	2 ½ tsp. baking powder
1 ½ tbs. grated orange rind	½ tsp. salt
¾ cup orange juice	¾ cup chopped nut meats

Cream the shortening and honey well. Add the beaten egg and orange rind. Sift the dry ingredients and add alternately with the orange juice. Add chopped nuts. Pour into greased loaf pan, the bottom of which has been lined with waxed paper.

Bake at 325° F. for 1 hour or until loaf is nicely browned and begins to shrink from the pan.
Yield: 1 loaf.

. . . SOYA BREAD . . .

2 ¾ cups milk, scalded	3 tsp. salt
1 tbs. honey	2 tbs. fat
2 cakes compressed yeast	½ cup sifted soya flour
1 tbs. sugar	8 ¼ cups sifted flour

Cool ½ cup of the milk to lukewarm, and soften the yeast in it. Pour remainder of milk, while still hot, over honey, sugar, salt and fat, then cool the mixture. Mix soya and all but ½ cup of the flour. Stir in liquid ingredients, mix thoroughly. Knead on a slightly floured board, working in as much of the unused flour as needed to make the dough soft, smooth, and elastic.

Let dough rise in a warm place until double in size. Punch it down to let out some of the gas, turn dough upside down, and let it rise again to double its size. Punch it down again, divide into thirds, mold into loaves, and place in 3 greased bread pans. Let rise until double in size.

Bake in a moderately hot oven (385° F.) for 15 minutes, then at moderate heat (350° F.) for the rest of the time. Bake 45 minutes to 1 hour, or until bread shrinks from sides of pans.

. . . WHOLE WHEAT BREAD . . .

2 cups lukewarm milk or 1 cup milk and 1 cup water	¼ cup honey
1 tbs. salt	1 cake compressed or dry yeast
¼ cup shortening	5 ½ cups (about) whole wheat flour, finely ground

Follow same directions as for Enriched Bread, except that you do not sift whole wheat flour. Mix with a spoon for a few minutes to lighten the flour. Bake at 375° F. in 2 greased bread pans for about 45 minutes or until nicely browned and loaves shrink from sides of pans. Another way to test if bread is done is to tap it; if it sounds hollow it is done. For a soft crust, top with butter before baking.

For faster rising, use two yeast cakes instead of one.

. . . HONEY WALNUT BREAD . . .

½ cup coarsely chopped walnuts	1 egg, beaten
2 cups sifted flour	½ cup honey
3 tsp. baking powder	½ cup milk
½ tsp. salt	2 tbs. melted butter

Combine all the dry ingredients and add the nuts. Combine the egg, honey, milk and butter; mix well and add to the first mixture. Stir until the ingredients are just moistened.

Bake in a greased bread pan in 350° F. oven for 45 to 50 minutes or until nicely browned.

. . . CORN GEMS . . .

2 ½ tsp. baking powder	2 eggs
1 tsp. salt	1 ¼ cups milk
1 ¼ cups sifted flour	3 tbs. honey
1 cup corn meal	¼ cup melted shortening

Add baking powder and salt to sifted flour and sift again. Add corn meal and mix well.

Combine well-beaten eggs, milk, honey and melted shortening. Add to dry ingredients; mix well. Bake in well greased baking pan in hot oven (400° F.) 30 minutes, or until done. Cool, cut into small squares. Serve with butter.

. . . HONEY ALL-BRAN UPSIDE DOWN MUFFINS . . .

2 cups All-Bran	1 cup sifted flour
½ cup honey	1 tsp. baking soda
1 ¼ cups milk	½ tsp. salt
1 egg, slightly beaten	¼ cup honey
½ cup currants	

Combine All-Bran, honey and milk; let stand until most of moisture is taken up. Stir in egg.

Sift together flour, soda and salt; add to All-Bran mixture, stirring *only until combined.*

Put 1 teaspoon honey into bottom of each greased muffin cup; sprinkle with about 1 teaspoon currants. Fill 2/3 full with batter.

Bake in moderately hot oven (400° F.) about 25 minutes. Let stand about 5 minutes before removing from pans. Serve currant side up.

Yield: 12-15 muffins, 2½ inches in diameter.

. . . BRAN PEANUT BUTTER MUFFINS . . .

1 cup milk	3 tbs. peanut butter
1 cup whole bran cereal	1 egg
5 tbs. shortening	1 cup flour
1 tbs. honey	3 tsp. baking powder
	¾ tsp. salt

Pour milk over bran cereal; let stand 5 minutes. Cream shortening, honey and peanut butter together. Add egg. Beat well. Add bran mixture. Sift flour, baking powder, salt, and add to bran mixture, stirring only until dampened. Fill greased muffin pan two-thirds full; bake in hot oven (400° F.) 25 minutes.

Yield: 12 large muffins.

. . . GINGER-HONEY-PEANUT MUFFINS . . .

3 tbs. butter or margarine	½ tsp. salt
2 tbs. honey	2 tsp. baking powder
1 egg, well beaten	¼ tsp. soda
1 ½ cups sifted flour	⅔ cup milk
1 tsp. cinnamon	½ cup honey
½ tsp. ginger	1 cup chopped peanuts

Cream butter, add honey and beat until fluffy. Stir in egg. Sift flour, measure and sift with the cinnamon, ginger, salt, soda and baking powder and add alternately with milk and honey mixture. Stir in peanuts and bake in well greased muffin pans at 350° F. 20 to 25 minutes.

Makes about 12 muffins.

. . . HONEY-NUT WHEELS . . .

Favorite pastry recipe using 2 cups flour.

3 tbs. soft butter or margarine	⅛ tsp. nutmeg
4 tbs. honey	½ cup coarsely chopped nuts
1 tbs. cinnamon	½ tsp. grated orange or lemon rind

Roll out dough until about ¼ inch thick; spread with butter and honey, sprinkle with cinnamon, nutmeg, nuts and rind in the order named. Roll up like jelly roll and cut into ½ inch slices. Place sliced side down on greased muffin tins or baking sheet. Bake in moderate oven (350°) about 15 minutes or until nicely browned.

Makes about 12 depending on thickness.

. . . RAISIN BANANA MUFFINS . . .

1 cup seedless raisins	¼ cup melted shortening
1 egg	2 cups sifted all-purpose flour
½ cup mashed banana	3 tsp. baking powder
½ cup sour milk or buttermilk	¼ tsp. soda
¼ cup honey	1 tsp. salt

Rinse and drain raisins. Beat egg and add bananas, milk, honey, shortening and raisins. Sift together flour, baking powder, soda and salt, and add to first mixture all at once, stirring only until moistened. Fill greased muffin pans 2/3 full. Bake in hot oven (400° F.) 20 to 25 minutes. Serve hot.

Makes about 15 medium-sized muffins.

Sauce:

3 cups cut rhubarb	Honey to taste
¼ cup water	3 drops red vegetable coloring

Roll:

2 cups flour, sifted	4 tbs. shortening
2 tsp. baking soda	2 tbs. honey
1 tsp. salt	⅔ cup milk

1 tbs. melted shortening

Cook rhubarb in water until soft (about 5 minutes). When almost cool stir in honey to sweeten and add coloring.

Sift flour, baking soda and salt. Cut in shortening. Blend honey with milk and add enough to make soft dough. Turn on floured board and knead gently a few minutes. Roll out into rectangular sheet about 8 inches long by ¼ thick. Brush with melted shortening.

Roll up loosely as for jelly roll. Cut into 1 inch slices; place slices cut side down on greased muffin pans and bake in 400° F. oven 15 to 20 minutes or until golden brown. Serve warm with rhubarb sauce poured over each roll.

Makes from 10 to 12 rolls.

SOUPS AND MACARONI

. . . BLAABAER SUPPE . . .
Norwegian Blueberry Soup

1 ½ cups blueberries, washed	2 tbs. cornstarch mixed with
1 quart water	2 tbs. water

3 tbs. honey

Wash fresh blueberries. Place them in a saucepan with water. Bring to a boil and simmer until berries are very soft. Strain the berries and the juice through a sieve and return the mixture to saucepan. Mix cornstarch with 2 tablespoons cold water and stir into the soup. Add honey and heat to the boiling point, stirring constantly with a wooden spoon, let boil for 2 or 3 minutes.

Serve hot or chilled.

Serves 4.

. . . HEDELMAKEITTO . . .
Cold Finnish Fruit Soup

1 lb. mixed dried fruit	1 stick cinnamon
3 tart apples, diced	3 tsp. cornstarch or
2 tbs. honey	potato starch
1 ½ quarts water	3 tbs. cold water

Wash dried fruit in warm water. Drain. Soak in water overnight or for 3 hours. Cook in same water 15 minutes. Add apples, honey and cinnamon. Dissolve cornstarch in 3 tablespoons cold water. Add to mixture and cook about five minutes or until slightly thickened.

Cool and serve. Serves 4-5. Serve with krisps.

May be served as a soup or dessert.

. . . LOBSTER BISQUE . . .

1 6½ oz. can lobster	1 bay leaf
(or 1 cup fresh)	1 tsp. honey
1 small onion, finely minced	½ tsp. salt
2 tbs. butter	Pepper
2 cans tomato soup	½ cup light cream (optional)
or consommé	⅓ cup sherry wine or rum
½ tsp. whole cloves	

Flake lobster. Sauté onion in butter until golden brown. Add

tomato soup, cloves, bay leaf, honey, salt and pepper. Simmer slowly for 20 minutes, covered. Remove cloves and bay leaf, add lobster and cream and heat to boiling point. Just before serving add sherry or rum.
Serves 4.

. . . SPAGHETTI MARINARA . . .
Spaghetti with Mariner Sauce

1 lb. spaghetti	2 filets of anchovy
2 sliced onions	Salt and pepper to taste
1 clove garlic	1 tsp. honey
4 tbs. olive oil	½ tsp. orègano
1 large can plum tomatoes	2 oz. grated Romano cheese

Sauté onion and garlic in hot oil about 5 minutes or until soft; remove garlic; add tomatoes; cook rapidly for 5 minutes; then lower flame and simmer covered for 1 hour. Add anchovies cut into small pieces. Use very little salt and pepper; add honey. Cook slowly for 10 minutes. Add oregano; stir. Keep hot over very low flame until ready to serve.

Cook spaghetti as usual. Drain; arrange on hot platter and pour sauce over spaghetti. Sprinkle with grated cheese.
Serves 4.

NOTE: This sauce may be used with boiled rice; on pizza, and baked fish.

The honey neutralizes the acid in the sauce and makes it more digestible to many people.

. . . FUSILLI WITH CAULIFLOWER . . .

1 small cauliflower	1 tbs. pignoli (pine nuts)
4 tbs. olive oil	1 tbs. currants
1 large minced onion	Salt and pepper to taste
3 filets of anchovy	1 lb. fusilli (pasta)
1 No. 2 can tomatoes	1 tsp. honey

45

Wash and break or cut cauliflower into small pieces. Cook in rapidly boiling salted water about 12 minutes or until tender but not soft. Drain; set aside.

Heat oil in saucepan; add onion; cook 3 minutes or until almost soft. Cut up anchovies; add; stir about 2 minutes or until dissolved. Add tomatoes; cover; simmer 20 minutes. Add cauliflower, pine nuts, currants, honey and very little salt and pepper. Mix well; keep hot over very low flame.

Boil fusilli according to directions on package. Drain. Mix in casserole or bowl with cauliflower mixture; top with grated cheese if desired, but this is usually served without cheese. Serve hot.

Serves 4 to 6.

Any type pasta, or macaroni such as spaghetti, shells, elbows, bows or noodles may be used.

GAME, FOWL AND SEA FOOD

. . . BRANDIED DUCK . . .
(Anitra al Cognac)

1 duck (6 lbs.)	Pinch of thyme
Salt and pepper to taste	1 clove garlic
2 large onions, chopped	3 jiggers cognac
2 tsp. chopped parsley	1 pint claret
1 bay leaf	¼ cup olive oil
½ pound mushrooms	1 tbs. honey, thyme honey preferable

Have duck cleaned and cut into serving pieces. Dry. Sprinkle lightly with salt and pepper. Put in deep enamel dish. Add onions, parsley, bay leaf, thyme, garlic, cognac, and claret. Cover. Marinate for 4 hours, or overnight in cool place.

Put oil in earthenware casserole; heat over high flame. Brown duck in oil for about 12 minutes on both sides after it has been drained and dried on a towel. Then add marinating liquid, honey and sliced mushrooms. Cover; simmer over low flame for 1 hour or until duck is tender.

Serve hot. Enough for 4.

. . . PHEASANT, WILD RABBIT OR VENISON . . .

These may be prepared in the same way as for Brandied Duck.

. . . DUCKLING ORIENTAL . . .

1 can Mandarin Oranges	¼ tsp. pepper
(11 oz.) (and juice)	2 cloves garlic
1 duckling, 4 lbs.	¼ cup lemon juice
1 tsp. salt	2 tbs. honey

Cut duckling into quarters, sprinkle with salt and pepper, and place skin side up on rack in baking pan. Bake one hour in 325° oven. Arrange duckling, drained of fat, in shallow casserole. Mash garlic and add to orange segments, honey and juices. Pour over duckling, cover and continue baking for 30 minutes or until tender.

Serves 4. Serve with sautéed mushrooms.

. . . RABBIT SWEET AND SOUR . . .
(Coniglio-Dolce-Agro)

1 rabbit (3 or 4 lbs.)	Salt and pepper to taste
2 oz. olive oil (2 tbs.)	1 tbs. honey
1 tbs. chopped salt pork	1 tbs. wine vinegar
1 tbs. chopped parsley	1 cup dry sauterne
1 clove garlic, chopped	2 tbs. tomato paste
¼ tsp. crushed red	½ cup warm water
pepper seeds	2 tbs. pine nuts

2 tbs. raisins

Have rabbit cleaned and cut into small serving pieces.

Place olive oil and chopped salt pork in pot with parsley, garlic, and crushed pepper seeds. Add rabbit and brown well for about 30 minutes. Add salt and very little pepper, honey and vinegar; stir well. Pour ½ cup of sauterne over it. Cover; simmer 10 minutes. Add tomato paste blended in ½ cup of warm water. Lower flame; add nuts and raisins. Cover tightly; simmer about 20 minutes or until tender. Add remaining sauterne. Turn flame high; boil 1 minute.

Serve very hot. Serves 4 to 6.

. . . HUNG YUN GAI DING . . .
(Chicken with Walnuts)

1 cup shelled walnuts	1 tbs. flour
Deep fat	1 tsp. honey
1 cup diced chicken	½ tsp. salt
3 tsp. lard	2 tbs. soy sauce

1 cup sliced mushrooms

Fry walnuts in deep hot fat or oil until brown, about 3 minutes. Remove with perforated spoon and drain on brown paper. Cool.

Heat lard in skillet. Fry chicken 10 minutes, stirring to brown evenly. Mix flour, salt, and honey with soy sauce and combine until smooth. Stir into chicken. Add mushrooms; stir and cook 5 minutes. Cover pan, simmer 20 minutes or until chicken and mushrooms are tender. Remove from fire; fold in walnuts and serve hot.

Serves 2 to 3.

Toasted almonds may be substituted for walnuts.

. . . ANGUILLE MARINATE . . .
(Marinated Eels)

2 lbs. thick eels	Salt and pepper to taste
1 bay leaf	1 tsp. rosemary leaves

Have eels skinned, cleaned and cut into 2 inch pieces, by your fishman. Place in a large saucepan and cover with cold water. Add balance of ingredients and bring to a quick boil. Boil about 5 minutes or until meat when pierced with fork is tender. Drain and keep hot in covered saucepan.

Prepare the following marinade:

¾ cup vinegar	1 large onion, sliced
½ cup water	1 bay leaf
1 clove garlic, crushed	1 tsp. chopped fresh mint
2 tbs. oil or clarified butter	or ½ tsp. dry mint
1 tbs. honey	

Boil vinegar and water in a saucepan, 2 minutes. Add honey.

Sauté garlic and onion in oil or clarified butter. Add to hot vinegar mixture, add bayleaf and chopped mint. Simmer 5 minutes. Pour over hot drained eels. Let stand on hot stove about 10 minutes before serving. Serve hot.

This may also be served cold, with hot vegetables or salad.

This marinade is excellent on boiled or broiled, mackerel, whiting or bass.

. . . KRYDDESILD . . .
(Herring in Wine Sauce)

7 herrings (medium size)	2 tbs. water
1 large onion, sliced	1 tbs. tart wine
3 tbs. oil	1 tbs. honey
3 tbs. vinegar	½ tsp. pepper

6 whole cloves

Remove skin and bones from herring and soak in cold water for 2 hours. Then rinse in fresh water.

Mix onion with a blend of oil, vinegar, water, wine and honey. Add pepper and cloves.

Cut herring into small pieces and place a layer in glass jar. Over this put some of the onion mixture; alternate with herring and onion mixture until used up. Cover jar tightly and put in cool place for 24 hours before serving.

Serve on crackers or toast rounds.

. . . LOBSTER-RICE AU GRATIN . . .

1 6½ oz. can lobster	2 cups hot medium white sauce
(or 1 cup fresh)	with 1 tbs. honey
2 cups cooked rice	Salt and pepper
1 cup grated cheddar cheese	½ cup bread crumbs, toasted
1 tsp. grated onion	Paprika

Flake lobster, remove hard membrane. In a casserole arrange alternate layers of lobster and rice. Melt cheese in hot white sauce seasoned with grated onion, salt, pepper; pour over lobster and rice. Top with crumbs, sprinkle with paprika. Bake in moderate oven (350°) until top is brown, about 30 minutes.

Serves 4.

. . . TEN-DON . . .
(Fried Shrimp in Sauce)

1 lb. rice	2 carrots, diced
4 cups water	¼ cup soy sauce
1 lb. medium-sized shrimp	1 tbs. honey
3 tbs. fat or oil	½ tsp. salt

Boiling water

Wash rice in sieve under running water until water runs clear, and starch is removed.

Place rice, 4 cups water and salt in heavy saucepan with tight cover. Bring to a boil. Stir. Cover and cook over low heat for 25 minutes. Water should be absorbed by rice by this time. Remove from fire. Stir and keep in warm place.

Wash and shell shrimps; remove black vein and wash again. Drain and pat dry with absorbent paper.

Heat fat in skillet and fry shrimp until brown on both sides. Add diced carrots, soy sauce, salt, honey and enough boiling water to cover. Cover skillet and cook slowly until carrots are tender (about 15 minutes). Add cooked rice and serve hot in large bowls.

Serves 4 large portions.

. . . TROTA CON ACCIUGHE . . .
(Trout with Anchovy)

6 trout	4 filets of anchovy
Salt and pepper to taste	1 cup dry sherry or sauterne
1 cup flour	1 tsp. fresh mint (chopped)
6 tbs. olive oil	1 tsp. chopped parsley
3 tbs. butter	Juice of 1 lemon

Clean trout; dry with absorbent paper; salt and pepper to taste; roll in flour. Fry slowly in hot olive oil about 10 minutes or until brown on both sides.

Melt butter in saucepan over low flame. Add anchovy filets

cut into small pieces; cook about 5 minutes. Add sherry or sauterne, cover; simmer 1 minute. Add mint and parsley; simmer 3 minutes. Add lemon juice.

Place fish on hot platter; pour sauce over it. Serve very hot with favorite vegetables.

Serves 4 to 6.

. . . TUNA SWEET AND SOUR . . .

2 lbs. fresh tuna fish	6 tbs. wine vinegar
¼ cup oil	1 tsp. honey
2 large onions, sliced	Salt and pepper to taste

6 sprigs fresh mint or sweet basil, chopped

Have tuna sliced 1½ inches thick. Season with salt and pepper. Pour oil in skillet and brown fish on both sides, about 10 minutes. Remove fish. Set in warm dish and set aside. Cover.

Cook onion slowly in same oil remaining in skillet, if necessary add a little more. When onion is very soft but not brown, add vinegar, honey and chopped mint or basil. Cover and simmer 3 minutes. Replace fish in pan with sauce; cover and cook 5 minutes more. Serve very hot.

Serves 4-6.

Fish may also be served cold. Cool fish, cool sauce and pour sauce over fish. The longer it marinates the better the flavor.

. . . SWORDFISH SWEET AND SOUR . . .

Use same ingredients and directions as for Tuna fish, except substitute swordfish.

. . . SEAFOOD PIZZARETTS . . .

1 cup fresh crabmeat or a 6 oz. can of crabmeat	8 thin slices tomato
4 English muffins	1 teaspoon thyme, marjoran or oregano
2 tbs. honey	¼ cup butter or margarine
8 slices sharp cheese	Paprika

Remove hard membrane from crabmeat, if in can, and leave in chunks.

Spread split toasted muffins with honey. Place on each half a slice of tomato, a slice of cheese and some of the crabmeat. Sprinkle with herbs and paprika and top with butter. Place on cookie sheet and bake in moderate oven (350° F.) for 15 minutes or until cheese is melted. Serves 4. Good supper snack.

If desired, you may substitute boiled lobster, diced, or eight anchovy filets, cut into small pieces, for the crabmeat.

MEATS

. . . APPLE MEAT ROLL . . .

2 lbs. ground chuck or round of beef
Salt and pepper
2 eggs, slightly beaten
2 slices white bread, crumbled into small pieces
1 medium onion, chopped finely
½ tsp. dry mint leaves

2 cups finely chopped apples, peeled and pared
2 cups soft bread crumbs
1 tbs. lemon juice
1 tsp. grated lemon rind
¼ tsp. cinnamon
1 tbs. brown sugar
1 tbs. buckwheat honey

Mix ground beef with salt and pepper, eggs, crumbled bread, mint and onion. Blend well. Pat meat mixture into an oblong (10" x 14") ½" thick on waxed paper. Spread meat with mixture of chopped apples, soft bread crumbs, lemon juice, lemon rind. cinnamon, brown sugar and honey. Using waxed paper roll up as for jelly roll. Place into greased oblong pan and bake at 350° F. for 1 hour. Slice into 1" slices and serve hot, with glazed carrots and onions. Garnish with water cress or parsley.

Serves 6.

. . . GREEK BEEF STEW . . .
(Stifato)

1 ½ lbs. boneless beef	1 tbs. honey
(rump or chuck)	1 cup canned tomatoes,
1 lb. small onions	chopped
3 tbs. fat	2 cloves
1 cup hot water or broth	4 peppercorns
½ cup wine vinegar	Salt and pepper to taste

Have beef sliced like small cutlets about ½ inch thick. Brown quickly in fat on both sides. Remove from skillet. In the same fat brown onions, which have been left whole; add a little more fat if necessary. Combine with meat. Season.

Combine water or broth, vinegar, honey, cloves and peppercorns; heat thoroughly without boiling; add meat, onions and tomatoes. Cover skillet and cook over low heat until meat and onions are tender, about 50 minutes.

Serve hot.

Serves 3-4.

. . . HONEY HAM LOAF . . .

3 tbs. honey	¼ cup brown sugar
4 cups Corn Flakes	½ lb. ground lean pork
2 eggs, slightly beaten	½ lb. ground veal
1 tbs. prepared mustard	1 cup milk
1 lb. ground smoked ham	½ tsp. salt
2 tbs. chopped green pepper	

Spread honey in bottom of 9½ x 5¼-inch loaf pan; sprinkle evenly with brown sugar.

54

Crush Corn Flakes slightly; combine with remaining ingredients, mixing thoroughly. Pack lightly over honey mixture.

Bake in moderate oven (350° F.) about 1½ hours. Turn out, bottom up, on heated platter.

Yield: 8 slices, about 1 inch thick.

. . . BAKED HAM WITH APPLES . . .

2 ham slices (tenderized or precooked) about 1" thick	½ tsp. ground cloves
½ cup brown sugar, blended with 1 tbs. honey	3 cups apples, peeled, pared and cut into thick slices
	½ cup apple juice

To prevent curling, slash edges of ham slices and brown thoroughly on both sides in a skillet rubbed with oil. Mix brown sugar, honey and cloves. Place one ham slice in the bottom of a casserole. Place ½ of sliced apples over top of ham. Sprinkle with half the amount of brown sugar mixture. Place the other slice over apples and cover with the rest of the apples and brown sugar mixture. Pour apple juice over all. Bake covered in a 325° F. oven for 25 to 30 minutes.

Serve with broccoli, carrots and cranberry sauce.

Serves 4.

. . . BAKED HAM DE LUXE . . .

1 Ham	1 cup crushed pineapple
1 cup honey	¼ cup brandy
	cloves

Select ham of desired size. Place fat side up on a rack in an open pan. Bake in slow oven (325° F.) 20 to 25 minutes per pound.

About half hour before it is done, remove from oven. Remove the rind. Score fat in diagonal lines with a sharp knife. In each diamond place a whole clove. Combine honey and pineapple, and spread over ham. Return to oven and finish baking. Baste frequently.

About 10 minutes before its done pour brandy over the ham, and baste it once or twice

. . . SPICED BROILED HAM . . .

1 slice ham, precooked, 1 inch thick	½ tsp. ground cloves ¼ tsp. allspice
4 tbs. honey diluted with 1 tbs. lukewarm water	Dash of cinnamon 1 tbs. orange juice

Place ham slice on broiler rack.

Combine honey, water, spices and orange juice. Mix well and brush or spread half of mixture on top of ham slice. Place about 4 inches below flame and cook about 10 minutes or until nicely browned. Turn ham and brush balance of honey mixture on it. Continue cooking until brown and tender. Baste occasionally with the pan juice.

1 lb. boneless ham serves 3.

Serve with sweet potato puffs or candied carrots.

. . . MUSHROOM CHOP SUEY . . .

¼ cup butter or fat	1 tsp. salt
1 ½ cups (¾ lb.) beef tenderloin or lean veal, cut in thin strips	¼ tsp. white pepper 1 ½ cups hot water
1 cup chopped onion	1 cup canned or fresh mushrooms
2 cups diced celery	1 can bean sprouts (drained well)
	Sauce

Heat fat in skillet, add meat and sear quickly (without browning or burning). Add onion and sauté for 5 minutes. Add celery, salt, pepper and hot water. Cover and cook for 5 minutes; stir. Add mushrooms that have been sliced thinly. Add drained bean sprouts. Mix well and bring to a boil. Cover and cook 5 minutes. Add sauce. Mix lightly and cook another minute. Serve hot over rice.

Makes 4 to 6 servings.

If fresh mushrooms are used, wash, drain and slice with stems on. If butter is used, clarified butter does not turn brown.

SAUCE:

Combine 2 tbs. cold water with 2 tbs. cornstarch, 2 tsp. honey and 2 tsp. soy sauce. Blend thoroughly and add as above.

. . . MINTED LAMB CHOPS . . .

4 thick lamb chops
Salt and pepper to taste
¼ cup lukewarm water
½ cup honey

1 tbs. vinegar
2 tbs. chopped fresh mint leaves
  or 1 tbs. dried mint leaves

Combine all ingredients except lamb chops and salt and pepper, in a saucepan. Simmer 5 minutes.

Season lamb chops and place on broiler rack about 4 inches below flame. Broil 5 minutes on one side and brush with ½ of the mint sauce. Cook 5 minutes more. Turn chops and brush with balance of sauce and cook about 8 minutes under lower flame or until done to your taste. Baste occasionally with pan juice.

Four servings.

Serve with baked potato and tossed salad.

. . . POTATO-PORK PIE . . .

2 lbs. lean ground pork
1 tsp. salt
½ tsp. pepper
1 medium onion, grated or
  minced
2 tsp. mild honey
½ clove garlic, minced
½ tsp. thyme or marjoram

1 tbs. chopped fresh parsley
  or
½ tsp. dried parsley
¼ tsp. all spice
2 lbs. potatoes, peeled
⅓ cup warm milk or more
  if necessary
1 egg with 1 tbs. sharp
  grated cheese
2 tbs. butter

Combine and mix well all ingredients except last 4 ingredients.

Boil and mash potatoes with a little butter, salt and pepper to taste. Add warm milk; beat until fluffy.

Spread meat on bottom of baking dish or casserole; top with mashed potatoes.

Beat egg and grated cheese until frothy and pour over top. Bake at 350° F. for 40 minutes. Top should be nicely browned and meat cooked.

Serves 4 to 6.

. . . ROASTED SUCKLING PIG . . .

1 small suckling pig (about 10 lbs.)	1 tsp. thyme
	6 cloves garlic
Salt and pepper to taste	6 slices buttered toast, cubed
3 large navel oranges	Sage honey, ½ cup
3 large green apples	1½ cups wine, burgundy

Have suckling cleaned and slit down center for stuffing. Wipe with damp cloth. Rub lightly, inside and out, with salt and pepper. Peel and quarter oranges and apples; mix with thyme and bread cubes and stuff suckling. Sew or skewer together.

With point of sharp knife make 3 half-inch slits on each side; insert clove of garlic in each slit.

Roast in large pan in 450° F. oven for about 1 hour. When it begins to brown turn heat down to 375°. Baste with pan juice and cover suckling with brown paper or tin foil. Watch while cooking to make sure it doesn't get too dry; baste occasionally; if pan juices are not enough add a little hot water to pan. Cook about 3 hours. About 30 minutes before it is done remove pig from oven, take out garlic and rub all over with a blend of wine and honey to form a nice glaze. Put back in the oven and cook until done. If done, a large fork put through side of suckling will come out quickly.

Serve very hot in thick slices, with stuffed mushrooms and tossed green salad, or fruit salad with a tart dressing.
Serves 6 to 8.
At Christmas or New Years this was a must in our family.

. . . CHINESE ROAST PORK . . .

1 lb. boned shoulder pork (lean)	1 tbs. soy sauce
1 tsp. salt	¼ tsp. cinnamon
1 tbs. honey	¼ tsp. ground ginger

Combine all ingredients except pork. Brush on pork. Roast in hot oven one hour or until tender, basting from time to time with two extra tbs. of hot water mixed with 1 tsp. soy sauce.
Serves 4.

. . . SWEET AND SOUR PORK . . .

3 large green peppers	1 lb. lean pork
¾ cup shortening	1 cup chicken bouillon
1 small garlic clove, minced	4 slices canned pineapple
1 ½ tsp. salt	2 ½ tsp. cornstarch
2 large eggs	2 tsp. soy sauce
4 tbs. flour	⅓ cup vinegar
1/16 tsp. pepper	⅓ cup honey

Cut the large green peppers into six pieces each. Cook in boiling water until almost tender—about eight minutes. Drain.
Heat shortening in a heavy frying pan with one teaspoon salt and garlic.
Make a batter in separate bowl by beating together eggs, flour, ½ teaspoon salt and dash of pepper. Cut pork into ½ inch cubes; dip in batter. Separate pieces of pork with fork and drop one piece at a time into frying pan. Brown over a moderately hot flame until golden brown on one side—about 5 minutes. Turn pieces of pork over and brown on other side. Pour out all but one tablespoon of the fat. Add 1/3 cup chicken bouillon. Cut the pineapple slices in six pieces each. Add pineapple and

green peppers to pork. Cover pan tightly and cook over a very low flame for 10 minutes.

Blend together cornstarch, soy sauce, vinegar, honey and 2/3 cup chicken bouillon and add to mixture. Stir constantly until the juice thickens and the mixture is very hot—about 5 minutes. Serve immediately with hot, boiled rice.

Serves 6.

. . . SUB GUM CHOW MEIN . . .

3 tbs. butter or shortening	2 cups celery (cut in ½ inch pieces)
1 cup lean pork, cut in thin strips	1 ½ cups hot water
1 cup minced onions	1 can mixed Chinese Vegetables (drained well)
1 tsp. salt	3 cups boiled rice
Dash of pepper	

Sauce:

2 tbs. cold water	2 tsp. Soy Sauce
2 tbs. cornstarch	1 tsp. honey

Melt butter in hot skillet. Add meat, stir and sear quickly (without browning or burning), add onions and fry for 5 minutes. Add salt, pepper, celery and hot water. Cover and cook for five minutes. Add drained Chinese Vegetable. Mix thoroughly and heat to boiling point. Add sauce, cook 2 minutes more. Serve with hot boiled rice.

Serves 4 large portions.

. . . MARINATED SHISH KEBAB . . .

1 ½ lbs. lean lamb	2 medium-ripe tomatoes
¼ lb. mushrooms	Special Herb Sauce, or
2 small onions, sliced thick	Lemon Mint sauce
Salt and Pepper	

Have butcher cut lamb into 1¼ inch cubes. Wash, drain and cut mushrooms in halves. Cut each tomato in 6 wedges.

Roll lamb pieces, mushrooms and sliced onions in either of the above sauces and let stand for about 20 minutes.

Then put skewer through lamb cube, follow with a piece of tomato, a piece of mushroom and a slice of onion. Alternate until skewer is full, having piece of lamb at each end of skewer. These should fill 6 small skewers. Brush lightly with some of the sauce and season with a little salt and pepper.

Broil about 4 inches from flame, 10 minutes on each side or until the meat is browned and tender. Baste occasionally if getting too dry, with some of the sauce.

Serve hot on skewers with baked potatoes and carrots.

. . . SAUSAGE-SWEET POTATO CASSEROLE

½ lb. sausage	1 tbs. flour
2 medium-sized sweet potatoes	½ cup cold water
3 medium-sized tart apples	2 tbs. wild thyme honey
½ tsp. salt	1 tbs. sausage drippings

Cut link sausage into ½-inch pieces. Fry until well done. If bulk sausage is used, shape it into small balls before frying or break it up as it cooks. Save drippings.

Pare and slice potatoes and apples. Cover potatoes with cold water and par boil. Drain.

Mix salt, flour and water together and blend with honey until smooth.

Arrange layers of potatoes, apples and sausage in a small baking dish; pour some of the flour mixture over each layer. Top the dish with apples and sausage, and add drippings.

Cover; bake in a moderately hot oven (375° F.) until apples and potatoes are tender—about 45 minutes.

Serve with a crisp green salad.

Serves 2.

. . . GLAZED SAUSAGE WITH BURGUNDY . . .

2½ lbs. Italian sausage	½ cup burgundy
2 cups cold water	1 tbs. honey

Place cold water and sausage in skillet; boil briskly 3 minutes; lower flame; prick sausage with fork to allow fat to escape. Cook about 20 minutes or until all water evaporates and sausage is brown. Turn and brown other side 10 minutes or until done. Combine burgundy and honey; gradually pour it over sausage; cover and simmer 10 minutes longer.

Serves 4 to 6.

Serve hot with tossed salad, and garlic bread.

. . . FYLDT RIBBENSSETG . . .
(Fruited Spareribs)

2 strips spareribs (about 3 ½ lbs.)	2 tbs. orange blossom honey
	2 tbs. brown sugar
1 cup prunes	2 tbs. flour
1 cup pineapple, diced	⅛ tsp. cinnamon
4 apples	Salt and pepper

Soak prunes overnight. Pit and cut into small pieces. Pare and core apples and cut in eighths. Mix prunes, pineapple, apples, honey, sugar, flour and cinnamon.

Lay one strip of ribs on bottom of roasting pan; season with salt and pepper, top with the fruit filling, and cover with the other strip of ribs. Tie a cord around them, season and sprinkle with flour. Bake in a moderate oven (350° F.) for about 2 hours.

Serves 4. Serve with baked potato.

VEGETABLES, SAUCES AND MARINADES, VINEGARS

. . . HONEY BAKED BEANS . . .

2 large cans Navy, Kidney
   or Pea beans
6 slices bacon cut into
   1 inch pieces
½ tsp. salt, if necessary
2 tbs. catsup

¼ cup honey
2 tbs. brown sugar
1 tsp. ginger
½ tsp. dry mustard
1 medium sized onion, minced

Place half of beans drained, in a casserole or bean pot. Dot with half of bacon pieces. Combine balance of ingredients in the order given and mix. Place half over beans. Add rest of beans and balance of honey-onion mixture and top with remaining bacon. Cover pot and bake in slow oven at 325° F. for one hour.

To brown top, remove cover and bake until nicely browned, about 15 minutes. If beans are too dry, add a tablespoon or two of the bean liquid.

. . . TART RED CABBAGE . . .
(Rodkaal)

1 medium-sized head of red
   cabbage (about 2 lbs.)
Salt to taste

½ cup currant juice or vinegar
2 tbs. honey
1 tbs. caraway seeds

Wash cabbage and remove wilted leaves and core. Quarter and cook in rapidly boiling salted water about 20 minutes or until tender. Drain and shred. Set aside in covered pot on back of stove to keep warm.

Combine currant juice or vinegar and honey. Blend well and add to cabbage. Mix in seeds and keep warm until ready to serve.

Excellent with pork or sausages.

. . . SWEET SOUR CABBAGE . . .

4 cups shredded green or red cabbage	¼ cup honey
	¼ cup vinegar
½ cup diced bacon	½ cup water
3 tbs. flour	1 tsp. chopped onion

Cook shredded cabbage in boiling water until tender. Drain. Cook bacon until well done. Remove bacon from pan and place on cabbage. Blend bacon fat with flour. Add honey, vinegar, water and chopped onion. Cook until thickened. Pour over cabbage and bacon. Season to taste. Heat thoroughly. Serve hot. Serves 4 to 6.

. . . SICILIAN EGGPLANT RELISH . . .
(Caponatina)

2 medium-sized eggplants	2 oz. capers (washed)
½ cup oil	1 tbs. pine nuts
2 sliced onions, medium sized	2 tbs. honey
1 No. 2 can strained tomatoes	6 tbs. vinegar
1 cup diced celery	Salt and pepper to taste

Wash eggplants; dry with absorbent paper. Peel, dice into 1-inch cubes. Fry in hot oil about 10 minutes or until soft and slightly browned. Remove eggplant and put in large saucepan.

Fry onion in same oil about 3 minutes; add a little oil if necessary. When onions are golden brown, add tomatoes and celery; simmer about 15 minutes or until celery is tender. Add capers and nuts. Add this mixture to eggplant.

Blend honey and vinegar; add salt and pepper to taste; heat

slightly. Add to eggplant; cover; simmer about 10 minutes over very low flame. Stir occasionally to distribute flavor evenly. When done, place in bowl. Cool. Cover.

May be used as a side dish with meat or fowl; also as a sandwich filling or antipasto. Keeps for days in refrigerator. Serves 6 to 8.

. . . HARVARD BEETS . . .

1 can sliced beets or 1 lb. fresh beets sliced and boiled	¾ cup honey
	1 tbs. butter
1 tbs. cornstarch	3 whole cloves
½ cup wine vinegar	salt to taste

Dissolve cornstarch in vinegar and blend in honey. Add butter, cloves and salt and bring to a slow boil. Boil 5 minutes.

Arrange sliced cooked beets, that have been heated, in a covered dish; pour over the cornstarch mixture and let stand for about 20 minutes in a warm place.

Serve hot. Serves 4.

. . . HONEYED ACORN SQUASH . . .

2 Acorn Squashes	4 strips of raw bacon, cut
3 tbs. honey	into 1 inch pieces

Wash squash and cut in half lengthwise. Remove seeds. Pour one-fourth of the honey in each half and put a strip of bacon cut up over each half. Bake at 400° F. until squash is tender and bacon crisp.

Serve hot. Serves 4.

. . . GLAZED SWEETS . . .

Pare sweetpotatoes and cut in half; drop into enough boiling water (containing ½ teaspoon salt) to just cover. For each sweetpotato add 1 tablespoon honey and 1 teaspoon butter or margarine. Cover and boil until sweetpotatoes are tender. If liquid has not cooked down enough by the time they are tender, remove cover and boil rapidly until a syrup is formed. Baste sweetpotatoes occasionally with the syrup.

. . . SWEETPOTATO PUFF . . .

3 cups mashed sweetpotatoes	⅓ cup milk or orange juice
2 egg yolks, beaten	2 tbs. honey
2 tbs. fat or margarine, melted	½ cup seedless raisins
½ tsp. salt	2 egg whites beaten stiff

Combine sweetpotatoes, egg yolks, fat and salt. Beat. Combine milk or orange juice and honey and add gradually. Whip and add raisins. Whip again. Fold in stiff egg whites. Pile lightly into greased baking dish and bake in a moderate oven (350°) about 30 minutes or until puffed and browned.

Top with softened marshmallow, buttered bread crumbs or chopped nuts, if desired, before baking.

. . . SHERRIED SWEETS . . .

Proceed as for Sweetpotato puff, add ¼ cup dry sherry to mixture before baking.

. . . CANDIED SWEETS . . .

Slice or cut cooked sweetpotatoes in halves (6 medium-sized sweetpotatoes make 6 servings). Arrange in a shallow greased baking dish. Dot each half with fat; sprinkle with salt. Pour over the top ½ cup honey blended with 1 tablespoon brown sugar. Bake in a moderate oven (350° F.) 15 to 20 minutes, basting frequently with the honey. Or place under broiler until nicely glazed and browned.

. . . GLAZED CARROTS-ORANGE . . .

12 small carrots	¼ cup honey
¼ cup butter or margarine	1 tbs. brown sugar
1 large navel orange sections	

Cook scrubbed carrots in boiling salted water until tender. Drain. In a saucepan combine butter, honey and sugar. Heat until well blended. Roll carrots in mixture; simmer until carrots are nicely glazed and browned. Top with orange sections and simmer 5 minutes more or until orange sections are heated through.

Serve with ham or fowl.

. . . HONEY-CARROT RING . . .

2 tbs. plain gelatin
1 cup cold water
1 cup boiling water
¼ cup honey

½ cup lemon juice
½ tsp. salt
1 ½ cups (firmly packed)
grated raw carrots

Soften gelatin in ¼ cup cold water. Add boiling water, honey, ¼ cup cold water, lemon juice and salt. Chill until slightly thickened. Fold in carrots and turn into 1-quart ring mold. Chill until firm. Unmold on bed of crisp lettuce. Fill center of ring with cottage cheese, fruit or vegeatbles. Serve with French dressing or mayonnaise, if desired. Serves 8.

. . . GLAZED ONIONS . . .

12 small white onions
¼ cup honey

¼ cup butter

Follow same directions as for glazed carrots, without the brown sugar and orange. Peel outer thin skin off onions.

. . . SWEETPOTATO SOUFFLÉ . . .

4 eggs, well beaten
½ cup brown sugar
¼ cup margarine or butter, melted
4 large sweetpotatoes, grated
Grated rind of 1 lemon and 1 orange

1 cup milk, lukewarm
¼ cup honey
¼ tsp. clove
½ tsp. cinnamon
Salt

Combine and mix thoroughly first 5 ingredients. Blend milk with honey and beat into potato mixture; add spices and a dash of salt and beat again until fluffy.

Turn into a well greased baking dish and bake in 325° F. oven for about 1 hour, or until soufflé is firm and lightly browned. Serves 4 to 6.

. . . CANDIED TOMATOES . . .

6 large tomatoes (not too ripe)	¼ cup water
½ tsp. salt	2 tbs. butter
1 cup honey	

Place tomatoes, stem side down, in buttered baking pan. Mix honey, water and salt and pour over tomatoes. Put 1 teaspoon butter on each tomato. Bake at 350° F. 1 hour or until tomatoes are tender. Baste frequently. Add more water, if necessary.

. . . TOMATO SCALLOP . . .

2 cans tomatoes	2 tbs. butter or olive oil
½ tsp. salt	2 tbs. honey
Pepper to taste	1 cup bread or cracker crumbs

Cover bottom of small buttered baking dish with 1 cup of tomatoes. Sprinkle with salt and pepper and dot with some of the butter or oil, and one tablespoon of honey. Cover with half of the crumbs. Repeat with another layer of tomatoes, seasoning, butter and honey. Top with remaining crumbs. Bake 20 minutes in a hot oven 425° F. until nicely browned.

Four servings. Serve hot.

. . . ZUCCHINI SWEET AND SOUR . . .

6 medium-sized zucchini (Italian Squash)	2 tbs. honey
½ cup oil	1 tbs. chopped sweet basil
3 tbs. wine vinegar	Salt and pepper to taste

Wash and scrape zucchini lightly. Cut into lengthwise slices about 3/8 inch thick. Fry in oil about 3 minutes on each side until brown. Drain on absorbent paper. Sprinkle with salt and pepper. When all slices are done place in deep dish. Blend well the remaining ingredients and add to remaining oil in frying pan. Bring to a slow boil. Pour over zucchini. Sprinkle with additional chopped basil.

Serve hot or cold. Makes about 4 side-dish portions.

. . . ADANO'S BASTING SAUCE . . .

¼ cup olive or salad oil	½ cup Worcestershire sauce
¾ cup chopped onion	1 tbs. dry mustard
1 clove garlic, chopped	1 ½ tsp. salt
1 cup honey	1 tsp. oregano
1 cup catsup	1 tsp. black pepper
1 cup wine vinegar	½ tsp. thyme

Heat salad or olive oil in saucepan. Add chopped onion and garlic. Cook until tender. Add all remaining ingredients and bring to a boil, stirring constantly. Cook another 5 minutes, very slowly.

This all-purpose sauce can be poured into sterilized jars, sealed and stored. Makes 1 quart. Perfect for basting hamburgers, steaks, frankfurters, spareribs, chops, ham steaks and game.

. . . MINT MARINADE . . .

½ cup chopped fresh mint	¼ tsp. salt
2 tbs. clover honey	⅛ tsp. white pepper
1 cup cider vinegar	1 clove garlic, crushed

Put mint in a bowl. Blend honey with vinegar and add to mint. Add salt, pepper and garlic. Stir well.

Brush chops, flank steak and wild game with this marinade. Set meat aside for half hour. Then broil or roast as you prefer. Baste occasionally with marinade in pan to keep meat moist and juicy.

. . . LEMON-MINT SAUCE . . .

½ cup honey
½ cup lemon juice

¼ cup chopped fresh mint or
1 tbs. dried mint leaves
4 tbs. lukewarm water

Blend all ingredients, except mint, in a saucepan. Heat thoroughly over low flame. Mix in the mint.

Serve warm or cold with fish or lamb.

If served warm add a teaspoon of melted butter and heat thoroughly.

. . . SPECIAL HERB SAUCE . . .

2 tbs. chopped scallions
2 tbs. olive oil
2 tbs. chopped chives
2 tbs. chopped fresh tarragon leaves
3 tbs. chopped fresh parsley

3 tbs. clarified butter
½ lb. mushrooms, sliced
Pepper and salt to taste
½ cup bouillon or clear chicken broth
1 tbs. honey

1 tsp. Worcestershire sauce

Sauté scallions gently in olive oil until soft. Remove pan from fire; add chives, tarragon, parsley. Melt butter and sauté mushrooms quickly. Season; add herbs, bouillon and simmer for 5 minutes; stir in honey and Worcestershire sauce and simmer 2 minutes more.

Serve hot in sauce boat with broiled steak, chops or burgers. Good on broiled or boiled fresh tuna or swordfish.

. . . SEAFOOD SAUCE . . .

1 tbs. grated horse-radish
1 tsp. Worcestershire sauce
3 tbs. catsup

1 tbs. lemon juice or lime juice
1 tsp. honey
⅛ tsp. salt

Blend ingredients thoroughly in the order named. Excellent on crabmeat, lobster and shrimp cocktail.

70

. . . HONEY SOY SAUCE . . .

¼ cup honey
½ cup chicken broth, consommé
  or bouillon
¼ cup soy sauce

2 tbs. catsup
⅛ tsp. ground ginger
½ clove garlic, crushed

Combine all ingredients in saucepan, stir and cook over low heat 10 minutes. Makes 1 cup.

This is a delicious basting sauce, especially for ham, steaks, spareribs, frankfurters, hamburgers.

. . . HONEY TARTAR SAUCE . . .

1 cup mayonnaise
1 tsp. honey
1 tsp. minced olives
1 tsp. minced capers
  (optional)

1 tsp. onion juice
1 tbs. finely minced sweet pickles
1 tbs. lemon juice
2 tbs. chopped celery

Mix all of the ingredients until well blended. Keep in refrigerator in covered jar.

. . . VERMOUTH SAUCE . . .

½ cup olive oil
½ cup dry vermouth
1 tbs. crushed mint leaves

1 tbs. honey
⅛ tsp. pepper

Place all ingredients in a bowl and beat thoroughly until well blended.

Excellent on boiled fish, or broiled carp, salmon and pork chops.

. . . TARRAGON VINEGAR . . .

½ cup fresh tarragon leaves
1 cup wine vinegar

½ clove garlic, crushed
1 tbs. clover honey

1 clove

Crush tarragon leaves; place in glass jar; blend honey and vinegar and add with garlic and clove. Mix with a silver spoon and leave at room temperature to ripen. Keep tightly covered.

. . . BASIL VINEGAR . . .

Substitute sweet basil leaves for tarragon. Or 1 tbs. of dried basil leaves. Proceed as for Tarragon Vinegar.

. . . TARRAGON MARINADE . . .
(for Meat or Chicken)

½ cup olive oil	4 cloves garlic, crushed
3 tbs. tarragon vinegar	1 bay leaf
½ cup red wine	½ tsp. dry mustard
Juice and grated rind of 1 lemon	¼ tsp. salt
1 large onion, sliced	⅛ tsp. black pepper

1 tbs. honey

Beat the oil, vinegar, wine, lemon juice and rind together until nicely blended. Stir in balance of ingredients except the onion; place sliced onion in bottom of baking dish, put thick steak or quartered chicken over the onions and then pour over all, the marinade.

Turn meat or chicken occasionally so that marinade soaks through. Marinate for about two hours.

Baste with marinade while cooking your steak or chicken. If any is left over pour it over the meat when you serve it.

This is enough for a 4-pound chicken or 2 pounds of steak (broiled or baked).

Serve onion as side dish or add to a tossed green salad with french dressing.

. . . TIBERIUS PIQUANT SAUCE . . .

1 cup burgundy or dry sauterne	2 cloves garlic, chopped
1 cup olive oil and 2 tbs. honey	¼ cup wine vinegar
2 chopped onions, medium sized	⅓ tsp. dried red pepper seeds
Pinch of rosemary	¼ tsp. salt

Beat all ingredients except onion and garlic with egg beater until well blended. Then mix in onion and garlic. Store in jar for 24 hours. Remove garlic. Good with cold meats and fowl. Also may be used to baste meats and fowl while roasting or broiling. Adds exotic flavor.

Emperor Tiberius' chefs annointed his meats, game and suckling pigs with plenty of honey in this sauce.

SALADS AND

SALAD DRESSINGS

. . . AVOCADO-SEAFOOD SALAD . . .

2 medium-sized ripe avocados	1 cup flaked crab meat
1 cup diced celery	¼ cup Honey Roquefort Cheese
Lemon or lime juice	Dressing
	Paprika-Salt

Cut avocado into halves lengthwise; remove seeds and peel. Sprinkle with lemon or lime juice and salt to taste.

Combine diced celery, crab meat and dressing; blend lightly and fill centers. Top with paprika. Serve on crisp lettuce leaves. Serves four small portions.

Lobster, tuna, salmon, shrimp or any boiled flaked fish may be substituted for the crab meat.

. . . HONEY ROQUEFORT CHEESE DRESSING . . .

2 tbs. Roquefort cheese (crumbled)	1 tbs. mild honey
1 tbs. lemon juice	1 cup french dressing

Cream the cheese until smooth; combine with other ingredients and blend well. Store in covered jar in refrigerator.

Cheese should be at room temperature to cream well.

. . . BANANA FRUIT SALAD . . .

2 ripe bananas	4 fresh or canned peach halves
4 fresh or canned pear halves	8 fresh strawberries (or frozen)
2 large peeled oranges	Watercress
2 large sweet red apples	Lettuce

Honey Fruit Salad Dressing

Peel and slice bananas (to prevent from turning dark, sprinkle with a little lemon or grapefruit juice).

Slice oranges thinly crosswise; core and cut apples crosswise into 8 thick slices.

Arrange chilled lettuce leaves on cold plates.

Place fruit in the order named in circular pattern, on lettuce. Place 2 strawberries in center and garnish with watercress. Top with dressing.

Serves 4.

. . . BERMUDA SALAD BOWL . . .

1 small head cauliflower	⅔ cup celery-seed dressing
½ large Bermuda Onion	1 small head lettuce, shredded
½ cup shredded carrots	½ cup sharp cheese, crumbled

Separate cauliflower into flowerlets and slice them crosswise. Slice onion and separate into rings. Add carrots to cauliflower and marinate in dressing 30 minutes. Top with onion rings.

74

Before serving add shredded lettuce and cheese. Toss lightly and serve from salad bowl.

. . . CELERY-SEED DRESSING . . .

1 tsp. dry mustard	¼ medium onion, grated
1 tsp. salt	⅓ cup cider vinegar
½ tsp. paprika	1 cup salad oil
½ cup honey	1 tbs. celery seed

Measure dry ingredients into small bowl. Add honey and blend thoroughly. Add grated onion and small amount of vinegar. Beat mixture and add oil and remaining vinegar alternately; beat while adding. Add celery seed. Store in covered jar in a cool place.

. . . CHICKEN ALMOND SALAD . . .

1 cup roasted blanched almonds	1 tbs. honey
1 cup sliced celery	1 tbs. lemon juice
2 cups cubed cooked chicken	1 tsp. salt
¼ cup chopped pimiento	Watercress for garnish
¾ cup mayonnaise	Lettuce leaves

Chop almonds and combine with celery, chicken and pimiento. Blend mayonnaise, honey, lemon juice and salt and toss with chicken mixture. Arrange in salad bowl and garnish with watercress and halved seeded grapes or pineapple chunks if desired. Serve on lettuce leaves.
Serves 4 to 6.

. . . CRABMEAT SALAD PRIMAVERA . . .

1 6½ oz. can crabmeat	½ cup mayonnaise
1 tsp. finely-chopped onions	1 tbs. honey
1 tsp. finely-cut celery	2 tbs. lemon juice
2 tbs. finely-cut green pepper	1 tsp. horse-radish

Remove hard membrane from crabmeat, leave in fairly large

chunks. Add vegetables. Combine mayonnaise, honey, lemon juice and horse-radish. Add to salad and toss lightly. Arrange on platter in individual lettuce cups, garnish with stuffed or deviled eggs, asparagus tips, scallions and carrot sticks.
Serves 4.

. . . ITALIAN CITRUS SALAD . . .

3 large lemons	Salt and pepper to taste
3 large oranges	4 tbs. olive oil
1 tsp. chopped fresh mint	1 tsp. honey

1 head lettuce

Peel fruit and cut into sections. Place in salad bowl. Sprinkle with mint, salt and pepper. Pour olive oil and honey over fruit and mix thoroughly. Place on lettuce leaves and serve. Salad oil may be used if desired.
Serves 4 to 6.

. . . GRAPEFRUIT DELIGHT . . .

2 large ripe grapefruit	4 tbs. olive oil
1 large orange	1 tbs. orange blossom honey
1 large ripe lime	3 sprigs fresh mint, chopped
Lettuce leaves	Salt

Peel fruit. Separate sections; remove seeds and membrane from sections.

Place in bowl. Add mint and salt to taste; blend oil and honey. Mix gently; place in refrigerator and let it marinate 15 minutes.

Serve on chilled lettuce leaves.

This delightful and unusual luncheon salad serves 3 to 4.

For added zest top with mounds of chopped or diced cooked chicken mixed with a little french dressing.

. . . JELLIED FISH SALAD . . .

1 tbs. gelatin	1 tbs. honey
½ cup cold water	2 eggs, beaten
½ tsp. salt	2 cups cooked or canned flaked
½ tsp. celery seed	fish
¼ cup cider vinegar	Lettuce-Tomatoes-Cucumbers
¼ cup water	

Soak gelatin in cold water 5 minutes. Add seasoning, vinegar, honey, water and eggs. Stir well and cook over boiling water until thickened. Stir occasionally. Remove from fire.

Add flaked fish and mix well. Pour into individual molds or large ring or fish mold and chill. Unmold.

Serve on chilled lettuce leaves with quartered tomatoes and sliced cucumbers. Top with french dressing.

Three to 4 servings.

. . . HOT POTATO SALAD . . .

3 lbs. small potatoes	2 tbs. chopped pimiento
8 strips bacon, cut in ½-inch	2 tsp. salt
pieces	¼ tsp. pepper
⅔ cup honey mayonnaise	1 tsp. dry mustard
6 tbs. vinegar	½ tsp. sugar
⅔ cup diced celery	1 tomato, cut in wedges
6 tbs. chopped scallions	Salad greens
	Parsley

Scrub potatoes and cook until tender; peel and dice while hot. Sauté bacon until crisp and light brown; drain and add to potatoes. Combine mayonnaise, vinegar, celery, scallions, pimiento and seasoning; heat for 2 minutes over a low flame. Add to potatoes and bacon, mixing carefully so potato pieces are not broken. Arrange in salad bowl lined with salad greens. Garnish with wedges of tomato and parsley.

Yield: 6-8 servings.

. . . ITALIAN TOSSED SALAD . . .

½ head escarole
½ head chicory
¼ pound dandelion greens
¼ medium-sized cucumber
1 clove garlic

6 tbs. olive oil
1 tsp. avocado or mild honey
2 tbs. wine vinegar
Salt and pepper to taste

Peel and slice cucumber thinly. Remove outer leaves from all greens. Cut into 2-inch lengths. Wash thoroughly in cold water. Drain; dry.

Rub salad bowl with garlic. Put in mixed greens and sliced cucumber. Blend oil, honey, vinegar, salt and pepper and pour over salad. Toss and mix thoroughly.

Serves 6 to 8.

. . . TANGCOC GRAPEFRUIT SALAD . . .

3 peeled tangerines
1 large grapefruit, peeled
½ cup shredded coconut
(finely chopped)

3 tbs. of honey
diluted with 1 tbs. warm water
Toasted blanched almonds

Separate fruit sections and remove clinging strings and seeds. Roll each section in the honey mixture and then in the coconut.

Place on individual plates, on chilled lettuce leaves, by alternating 1 tangerine and 1 grapefruit section in the form of a swirl, to resemble a flower. Place a few almonds in the center of each serving.

If desired top with fruit salad dressing.

Serves 4.

No. 2 cans of tangerine and grapefruit sections may be used if desired.

. . . TOMATO-VEAL CUPS . . .

6 tomatoes	½ tsp. salt
1 ½ cups diced cooked veal	⅛ tsp. pepper
½ cup cooked peas	Honey mayonnaise
½ cup celery, coarsely chopped	6 slices toast
1 tbs. minced onion	Parsley, chopped

With sharp pointed knife, cut tops from tomatoes and remove pulp; turn tomatoes upside down to drain. Combine veal, peas, celery, onion, and season with salt and pepper. Add a little mayonnaise just to hold mixture together. Sprinkle inside of tomato cups with salt and pepper and fill with veal mixture. Top each with level teaspoonful of mayonnaise and broil 10 minutes to brown lightly. When browned, serve hot on toast. Garnish with parsley.

Yield: 6 servings.

. . . FROZEN TURKEY-PINEAPPLE SALAD . . .

1 ½ cups cooked diced turkey or chicken	1 cup chopped nut meats
	1 cup cream, whipped
¾ cup drained crushed pineapple	1 cup honey mayonnaise

Mix lightly in a bowl, the turkey, pineapple and nuts. Fold whipped cream in mayonnaise in a separate bowl and fold lightly into turkey mixture.

Turn into freezing tray with control set at coldest point. Freeze until ready to serve. Slice and serve on lettuce leaves with tomato wedges.

Serves 6 to 8.

. . . FROZEN FRUIT SALAD . . .

4 ounces cream cheese	1 cup pitted cherries
3 tbs. Avocado Mayonnaise	3 slices pineapple, cut into quarters
1 tbs. honey	½ pint (1 cup) whipping cream

Mix cream cheese with mayonnaise, add honey and mix until well blended. Add cherries and pineapple. Fold in whipped cream. Spoon in freezing tray. Freeze, but not too hard.

Serves 3-4. Serve on lettuce leaves and garnish with watercress or endive.

. . . AVOCADO MAYONNAISE . . .

½ cup orange juice	1 tsp. honey
1 tbs. lemon juice	½ tsp. salt
1 large ripe Avocado	

Combine all ingredients except avocado and beat until foamy. Peel and cut avocado in half. Remove seed. Mash to a pulp. Add honey-juice mixture a little at a time and beat until light and fluffy.

Makes about 1 cup of delicious dressing. Good on seafood and tart fruit salads.

. . . HONEY FRENCH DRESSING . . .

½ cup salad oil	½ tsp. paprika
½ cup lemon juice	½ tsp. salt
½ cup honey	1 clove garlic

Place ingredients in a tightly-covered pint jar and shake vigorously just before using.

Do not refrigerate.

. . . LEMON CREAM SALAD DRESSING . . .

3 tbs. honey	1 cup whipped cream
1 tbs. lemon juice	or
	whipped chilled evaporated milk

Combine honey and lemon juice, and whip until frothy; fold in whipped cream.

Serve immediately on fruit salads. Do not store because it separates.

80

. . . TROPICAL DRESSING . . .

1 egg	¼ cup orange juice
2 tbs. honey	1/16 tsp. salt
2 tbs. lime juice	2 heaping tbs. whipped cream

Combine and beat all ingredients until creamy, except cream; cook in double boiler until thick, stirring constantly. Remove; chill. Fold in whipped cream and serve. Excellent on fruit salad.

. . . FRUIT SALAD DRESSING . . .

½ tsp. dry mustard	3 tbs. orange blossom honey
½ tsp. salt	1 cup salad oil
½ cup lemon juice	2 tbs. orange juice

Mix mustard and salt; blend in lemon juice and honey. Slowly beat in oil; add orange juice; beat until smooth and creamy. Keep in refrigerator in covered jar when not in use.

. . . SPECIAL RUSSIAN DRESSING . . .

1 cup honey mayonnaise	3 tbs. chili sauce
2 chopped hard-boiled eggs	1 tbs. tarragon vinegar
12 sprigs chives, finely chopped	

Mix all ingredients in the order given until well blended. Keep in covered jar in refrigerator when not in use.

. . . HONEY MAYONNAISE DRESSING . . .

1 egg yolk	¼ tsp. dry mustard
½ tsp. salt	Pinch pepper and cayenne
1 tsp. honey	2 tbs. cider vinegar
1 cup oil	

Mix all ingredients together except the vinegar and oil. Add oil slowly and beat with rotary beater. Add vinegar and con-

81

tinue beating until thick and well blended. Store in covered jar in refrigerator.

. . . SOUR CREAM SALAD DRESSING . . .

1 tbs. honey	1 tbs. lemon juice
¼ tsp. salt	2 tbs. vinegar
Pinch pepper	½ cup sour cream, whipped

Blend ingredients in the order named, except whipped cream. Beat vigorously. Fold in sour cream. Serve on cabbage, cucumbers or lettuce. Good on boiled fish too.

. . . SWEET BASIL DRESSING . . .

3 tablespoons chopped sweet basil	¼ cup olive oil
	1 clove garlic
4 tablespoons wine vinegar	Salt and pepper to taste
1 tablespoon thyme honey	

Blend all ingredients thoroughly. Place in jar; keep in cool place, not cold. Allow to stand several hours before using. Use as needed.

Excellent on all vegetable salads, or orange and grapefruit salads.

. . . ZESTY DRESSING . . .

1 cup salad oil	1 tbs. Worcestershire Sauce
⅓ cup lemon juice	1 tsp. salt
3 tbs. honey	1 dash tabasco sauce
3 tbs. catsup	1 tsp. dry mustard
	1 tbs. grated onion

Combine all ingredients in a bowl and beat with egg beater until well blended. Or, place in blender and beat 2 minutes. Pour in jar and cover tightly.

. . . ZABEL'S CHUTNEY . . .

2 quarts sour apples	Juice of 2 lemons and the grated
2 green peppers	rind of 1
3 onions, medium	1 ½ cups vinegar
¾ lb. seedless raisins	¾ cup tart fruit juice
½ tbs. salt	¾ tbs. ginger
1 cup honey	¼ tsp. cayenne pepper

Wash and chop coarsely the fruit and vegetables. Add all other ingredients; stir and simmer until thick as chili sauce —about 30 minutes. Seal in hot, sterilized jars.

SALAD SUGGESTIONS

APPLE, DATE AND GRAPE SALAD:

Combine 2 cups diced apples, 1 cup seedless grapes and ½ cup chopped dates with your favorite honey dressing. Serve on chilled lettuce and garnish with parsley or watercress.

ORANGE AND PEAR SALAD:

Peel and section 3 oranges. Peel, core and dice 6 halves of pears, or use canned pear halves. Arrange on crisp lettuce and garnish with cherry and parsley, and fruit salad dressing.

CABBAGE AND APPLE SALAD:

Combine 2 cups shredded cabbage and 1 cup diced apples with your favorite salad dressing, enough to moisten. Serve on crisp lettuce and top with chopped nuts.
If desired add tomato wedges.

CARROT, APPLE AND RAISIN SALAD:

Combine 2 cups diced apple, ½ cup grated carrot, or shredded, and 1/3 cup of chopped raisins, with salad dressing to moisten. Serve on crisp lettuce with tomato wedges and watercress.

These salads serve 2 to 3. They are wonderful for your diet.

REFRIGERATOR CHEESE CAKES

AND TORTES

. . . MRS. NASSAR'S REFRIGERATOR CHEESE CAKE . . .

Crumb Topping:

Combine 2 tablespoons melted butter, 1 tablespoon sugar, ¼ cup finely chopped nuts, 2/3 cup graham cracker crumbs, ¼ teaspoon cinnamon and ¼ teaspoon nutmeg. Line bottom of 8-inch spring form pan or 8- or 9-inch square pan with waxed paper. Press crumb mixture in bottom of pan.

Cheese Filling:

2 envelopes unflavored gelatin	1 tsp. grated lemon rind
½ cup sugar	1 ½ lbs. creamed cottage
¼ tsp. salt	cheese, sieved
2 eggs, separated	1 tbs. lemon juice
1 cup milk	1 tsp. vanilla
½ cup orange blossom honey	1 cup heavy cream, whipped

Combine gelatin, ¼ cup of sugar and salt in top of double boiler. Beat egg yolks, milk and honey together; add to gelatin mixture. Cook over boiling water, stirring constantly, until gelatin dissolves and mixture thickens, about 10 minutes. Remove from heat. Add lemon rind. Cool. Stir in sieved cottage cheese, lemon juice and vanilla. Chill, stirring occasionally, until mixture mounds slightly when dropped from a spoon. Beat egg whites until stiff, but not dry. Gradually add remaining ¼ cup sugar and beat until very stiff. Fold into gelatin-cheese mixture with whipped cream. Turn into prepared pan and chill until firm (about 3 hours or more). Invert on serving plate. Carefully remove waxed paper. Garnish with maraschino cherries if desired. Makes 10 to 12 servings.

. . . REFRIGERATOR HONEY FRUIT CAKE . . .

1 ½ cups seedless raisins
½ cup dried apricots
2 cups orange juice
1 cup dried prunes, without pits
1 ½ cups cut candied cherries, pineapple and citron
1 tsp. orange peel, grated
1 tsp. grated lemon peel
½ cup margarine or butter
½ cup honey
½ cup confectioners sugar
½ tsp. salt

¼ tsp. mace
½ tsp. allspice
¼ tsp. clove
1 tsp. cinnamon
1 tsp. rum flavor or vanilla
2 cups zweibach crumbs, rolled fine
3 cups graham cracker crumbs, rolled fine
½ cup coarsely chopped toasted nuts

Rinse and drain raisins and apricots. Place in large bowl.

Heat orange juice to boiling point and pour over fruit. Cover bowl and let stand until cool. Then drain out excess orange juice, and set juice aside.

Cut apricots and prunes into small pieces. Combine all of the fruit and peels.

Cream margarine or butter with honey and sugar; mix in the salt, spices and flavoring. Add this to the fruits and let mixture stand about 3 hours. Then mix in the crumbs and chopped nuts.

Line two loaf pans with waxed paper and pack mixture into these. Chill in refrigerator 2 or 3 days before cutting.

Makes about 4 pounds of fruit cake, that will last fresh for months if wrapped in tin foil or heavy waxed paper.

. . . FROZEN LIME PIE . . .

6 eggs, separated	Grated peel of two limes
½ cup sugar	Juice of three limes
½ cup mild honey	2 cups heavy cream, whipped

1 ⅔ cups chocolate wafer crumbs

Combine egg yolks, sugar, honey, lime peel and juice in top of double boiler. Cook over hot water, stirring, until slightly thickened. Cool.

Fold in stiffly beaten egg whites. Fold in whipped cream. Sprinkle half of the crumbs into large refrigerator tray or 2 small ones. Pour in lime mixture. Top with remaining crumbs. Freeze until firm.

Makes 10 to 12 servings.

. . . LADY TANGERINE TORTE . . .

Grated rind of one large tangerine	2 oz. marshmallows (cut into small pieces)
1 ¼ cup tangerine juice (about 10 tangerines)	Sections of 1 large tangerine (cut into small pieces)
1 tbs. gelatin	1 cup heavy cream, whipped
½ cup honey	24 lady fingers

½ cup fresh strawberries

Add rind to juice. Soften gelatin in half cup of the juice and heat slowly until dissolved. Add honey and blend.

To the remaining juice, add marshmallows and tangerine sections.

Combine gelatin mixture with marshmallow mixture. Mix. Chill until it begins to thicken. Fold in whipped cream.

Line a 2-quart mold with lady fingers, which have been cut

in half, crosswise. Spoon in part of the gelatin, then place another layer of lady fingers over it and alternate with gelatin and lady fingers until they are all used up. Chill until firm. Then unmold and garnish with chilled strawberry halves.

Makes 8 portions

. . . HEAVENLY LEMON CHIFFON PIE . . .

1 tbs. gelatin	½ tsp. salt
¼ cup cold water	½ cup lemon juice
4 eggs, separated	1 tsp. grated lemon peel
¾ cup honey	1 cup heavy cream

Baked 9-inch pie shell

Soften gelatin in cold water. Combine the slightly beaten egg yolks, ¼ cup of the honey, salt, lemon juice and grated lemon peel in the top part of a double boiler. Place over boiling water and cook until of custard consistency, stirring constantly. Add softened gelatin and stir to dissolve. Remove from heat and cool until mixture begins to thicken.

Beat three of the egg whites until stiff and gradually beat in ¼ cup of the honey. Fold into the custard mixture and turn into baked pastry shell. Chill until firm.

Beat the remaining egg white until stiff and gradually beat in 2 tablespoons of the remaining honey. Whip the cream until stiff while gradually adding the remaining 2 tablespoons of honey. Combine with the sweetened egg white and spread on pie just before serving.

Makes one 9-inch pie.

. . . LEMON SNOW TART . . .

Filling:

1 tablespoon gelatin	½ cup boiling water
¼ cup cold water	1 tsp. grated lemon rind
⅓ cup lemon juice	½ cup honey

1 ½ cups sour cream

Sprinkle gelatin over combined cold water and lemon juice. Let stand for about 10 minutes. Add boiling water and stir until gelatin is dissolved. Add lemon rind and honey and mix well. Cool. Add sour cream and stir until blended. Whip 1 minute, with fork or whisk.

Chill until mixture is almost set. Then beat with rotary beater until light and foamy. Pour into Zweiback Honey Crust. Chill until set.

Yield: one 9-inch pie or 6 small tarts.

Zwieback Honey Crust:

2 cups fine Zwieback crumbs (about 1 6-oz. package)	½ cup melted butter or margarine
	3 tbs. honey

Mix crumbs, butter and honey. Press mixture in bottom and around sides of 9-inch pie pan or 6 small tart pans, using back of spoon or fingertips. Bake in a moderate oven (350° F.) for about 10 minutes. Cool.

. . . SICILIAN CREAM TORTE . . .

1 ½ lbs. ricotta (Italian cottage cheese)	2 squares bitter chocolate, chopped
¼ cup sugar	2 tsp. almond extract
2 tbs. orange blossom honey	1 spongecake (10-12 inches in diameter)
¼ pound glazed mixed fruit	

Strain ricotta through wire sieve to refine. Add sugar and honey; beat. Add chocolate and almond extract; blend until custard-like consistency is obtained. Set aside in cold place until ready to serve.

Cut plain spongecake in three layers. Put bottom layer in large round dish. Spread about ½ inch thick with filling. Top this with another layer of cake, then another ½ inch of the filling. Top layer should be spongecake. Set in refrigerator until this frosting is ready:

1 egg white	1 tsp. almond extract
1 ¼ cups sifted confectioners'	1 tbs. honey
sugar	½ tsp. lemon juice

Gradually mix ¼ cup of sugar with egg white. Beat in 1 tablespoon of honey; beat with spoon until smooth. Add flavoring and lemon juice; blend with more sugar (about ½ cup) until thick enough to spread.

Cover sides and top of Torte evenly. Place cherry in center. Distribute glazed fruit on top to form an attractive design.

Serves 10 to 12

BAKED CAKES, PIES AND COOKIES

. . . BAVARIAN CHEESECAKE . . .

2 eggs	½ tsp. vanilla
⅓ cup honey	1 tbs. butter
⅓ cup sugar	1 ¼ cups warm milk
1 tbs. flour	1 unbaked 9-inch pastry shell,
1 ½ cups pot cheese	chilled
½ tsp. salt	Nutmeg

Beat eggs and honey lightly in large bowl. Mix together sugar and flour and add. Add pot cheese, salt and vanilla. Melt butter in warm milk and add. Pour mixture into chilled unbaked pastry shell. Sprinkle top with nutmeg. Bake at 400° F. for 10 minutes, then at 350° F. until set—about 40 minutes. When a silver knife is inserted it should come out clean.

. . . COUSIN TESS' CHEESE CAKE . . .

Crust:

1 ½ cups zweiback crumbs
½ cup butter, softened
¼ cup sugar

½ cup finely chopped almonds
  or filberts
1 cup finely chopped coconut
  (8 ozs.)

Filling:

6 eggs, separated
½ cup sugar

⅓ cup clover honey
Rind of 1 lemon, grated

1 ½ lbs. cream cheese, mashed

In a bowl, mix all the crust ingredients until well blended, in the order named. Butter thickly the bottom and sides of a 9-inch, spring form pan. Line the bottom and sides with the crumb mixture.

In another bowl beat the egg yolks until thick and lemon-colored; gradually beat in honey and beat until light and fluffy. Add lemon rind and mashed cream cheese, beating until smooth. Beat egg whites until stiff; gradually add sugar and continue beating until very stiff and satiny. Fold into cream cheese mixture. Pour into crumb lined pan.

Bake in 350° F. oven about 50 minutes, or until mixture is lightly browned and slightly set in center. Remove to rack and allow to cool in pan; then loosen edges of crust from pan with spatula; release spring and remove outer rim. Serve cool. Serves 8.

. . . HONEYED APPLE PIE . . .

Pastry for 9-inch two-crust pie
6 large green apples
½ tsp. cinnamon
½ tsp. nutmeg
½ cup sugar, or more to taste
  if apples are very tart

2 tbs. orange blossom honey
1 tbs. brandy (optional)
Juice of 1 small lemon
Butter or Margarine

Peel, core and slice apples thickly. Mix in lemon juice. Combine spices and sugar and add.

Line pie pan and pile in apple mixture.

Combine honey and brandy and drizzle over apples. If apples are too juicy sprinkle a scant tablespoon of flour over all. Dot with butter or margarine and cover with top crust. Moisten edges, press together with tines of fork or flute with fingers. Slit top crust here and there with sharp pointed knife.

Bake at 425° F. about 45 to 50 minutes, or until apples are done and crust is golden brown. If crust browns too fast cover with brown paper. Serve warm or cold. Plain, with whipped cream or ice-cream. Serves 8.

. . . PINEAPPLE CHEESE PIE . . .

1 9-ounce can crushed pineapple
⅓ cup orange blossom honey
1 tbs. cornstarch
1 8-oz. package cream cheese, softened at room temperature
½ teaspoon salt

⅓ cup sugar
2 eggs
½ cup milk
½ tsp. vanilla extract
1 9-inch unbaked pastry shell
¼ cup chopped nuts

Cook pineapple with honey and cornstarch until mixture is thick and clear. Cool. Blend cheese, salt and 1/3 cup sugar. Beat in eggs one at a time. Add milk and vanilla. Spread pineapple mixture in pie shell. Pour in cheese filling; sprinkle with nuts. Bake 10 minutes at 400° F. then 40 minutes at 325° F. or until filling is firm but not dry.

Use flaky pie crust recipe or your favorite pie crust recipe. Serves 6 to 8.

. . . HONEY-BLUEBERRY PIE . . .

Flaky Pastry for Two-Crust Pie

3 cups berries	½ tsp. cinnamon
⅓ cup honey	1 tbs. butter
2 tbs. cornstarch or	1 egg white, lightly beaten
4 tbs. flour	

Prepare crust for 9-inch pie.

Pick over and wash berries. Brush bottom crust with egg white. Place on 9-inch pie pan and add berries. Add a little honey to cornstarch and blend well. Add remainder of honey; mix and pour over the berries. Sprinkle the cinnamon over all and dot with bits of butter. Cover with criss-cross pastry, or whole piece, with whole in center made with biscuit cutter to allow steam to escape.

Bake in hot oven (450° F.) 10 minutes. Reduce heat to 350° F. and bake 30 minutes longer or until filling is firm and crust is nicely browned.

Serves 6 to 8.

. . . STRAWBERRY PIE . . .

Substitute washed and hulled strawberries and add an extra tablespoon of honey. Proceed as above.

. . . BLACKBERRY PIE . . .

Substitute washed and drained blackberries and add an extra tablespoon of honey. Proceed as above.

. . . DOWN YONDER RAISIN PIE . . .

1 cup seedless raisins	1 cup dark honey
3 tbs. butter or margarine	¼ tsp. salt
½ cup brown sugar (packed)	2 tbs. cider vinegar
3 eggs	Pastry for single 9-inch crust

Rinse raisins and drain thoroughly. Cream together butter and sugar. Blend in lightly beaten eggs, honey, salt, vinegar and raisins. Pour into pastry-lined pie pan. Bake in hot oven (400° F.) 10 minutes. Reduce heat to moderate (350° F.) and bake 30 minutes longer, or until center is set.
Serves 6 to 8.

. . . GEORGIA PECAN PIE . . .

1 tbs. butter	⅛ tsp. salt
1 cup brown sugar	1 tsp. vanilla
1 cup buckwheat honey	1 cup pecans, broken coarsely
3 eggs, beaten	Flaky Pie Crust

Prepare crust and line 9-inch pie pan. Cream butter with sugar; add honey, eggs, salt and vanilla. Mix well. Fold in pecans. Turn into pastry lined pan. Bake at 400° F. for about 40 minutes, or until firm but not dry.
For special occasions top with whipped cream.
Serves 6 to 8.

. . . SOUR CREAM PRUNE PIE . . .

Pastry for Double Crust Pie

2 cups cooked prunes	⅔ cup sour cream
2 eggs	¼ tsp. salt
⅔ cup honey	1 tbs. lemon juice

Cut prunes from pits into large pieces. Beat eggs lightly and blend in the honey, sour cream, salt, and lemon juice until smooth and creamy. Add prunes. Pour into pastry-lined 8-inch pie plate. Cover with top crust. Flute edge and prick here and there with fork. Bake in 400° F. oven for 45 minutes or until golden brown.
Serves 6.

. . . AUNT SOFIA'S COFFEE CAKE . . .

1 ½ cups sifted flour
¼ cup sugar
2 tsp. baking powder
¾ tsp. salt
1 egg, beaten
⅓ cup milk
¼ cup honey

3 tbs. melted shortening
¼ cup drained, chopped
  cooked apricots or prunes
¼ cup margarine
⅓ cup honey
¼ cup shredded coconut
  or chopped nuts

Sift dry ingredients together. Combine egg, milk, ¼ cup honey and melted shortening. Mix and add to dry ingredients. Mix until smooth.

Pour batter into greased 8-inch square pan, 2 inches deep. Spread cooked fruit over batter. Cream margarine and honey, and spoon over fruit. Sprinkle with coconut or chopped nuts. Bake in 400° F. oven for 30 minutes or until done. Serve hot or cold.

Serves 6 to 8.

. . . MRS. KISTLER'S CHOCOLATE CAKE . . .

3 squares unsweetened
  chocolate, melted
⅔ cup honey
1 ¾ cups sifted cake flour
1 tsp. soda
¾ tsp. salt

½ cup butter or other shortening
½ cup sugar
1 tsp. vanilla
2 eggs, unbeaten
⅔ cup water

Blend chocolate and honey; cool to lukewarm. Sift flour once, measure, add salt and soda, and sift together three times. Cream butter thoroughly, add sugar gradually, and cream together until light and fluffy. Add chocolate-honey mixture and vanilla. Blend. Add eggs, one at a time, beating thoroughly after each addition. Add flour, alternately with water, a small amount at a time, beating after each addition until smooth. Bake in 2 greased 9-inch layer pans in moderate oven (350° F.) 30 to

35 minutes. Spread Plain-Chocolate frosting between layers and on top and sides of cake.
Serves 8.

. . . HONEY LEMON CREAM LAYER CAKE . . .

Cake:

½ cup shortening	¾ tsp. baking soda
1 cup honey	½ tsp. salt
2 eggs	2 tbs. lemon juice
2 cups sifted cake flour	¼ cup milk

Cream shortening with honey until fluffy. Add eggs one at a time and beat well after each addition.
Sift together the flour, baking soda, and salt.
Add lemon juice to milk. Stir.
Combine sifted dry ingredients with creamed mixture alternately, and soured milk.
Pour into two greased 8-inch layer cake pans. Bake 25 to 30 minutes in a moderate oven (350° F.).
Serves 6.

Filling:

1 egg yolk	¼ cup water
4 tbs. sugar	¼ cup lemon juice
2 tbs. cornstarch	¼ tsp. grated lemon peel
¼ cup honey	1 tbs. butter

Beat egg yolk in top of double boiler. Combine sugar and cornstarch and mix into egg yolk and add remaining ingredients. Cook over boiling water until mixture is thickened, about 15 minutes, stirring frequently. Cool. Spread on layers and put them together. Top with maraschino cherries for added color and zest, or chopped nuts.
Use packaged lemon pudding if you desire, but reduce liquid by 2 tablespoons and add 2 tablespoons of honey.

. . . ORANGE-ALMOND CAKE . . .

½ cup fat
¼ cup sugar
½ cup honey
Grated rind of 1 orange
5 egg yolks

2 cups cake flour, sifted
1 tbs. baking powder
½ tsp. salt
½ cup milk
¼ cup ground almonds

Cream fat with sugar until fluffy; add honey and orange rind and mix well. Beat in egg yolks one at a time, beating thoroughly. Add dry ingredients alternately with milk and beat until smooth. Add nuts. Pour into greased 9-inch square pan, lined on bottom with brown paper, then greased again. Bake in moderate oven, 350° F., 40 minutes or until cake shrinks from sides of pan.

Serves 6 to 8.

. . . PLAIN HONEY CAKE . . .

2 cups sifted cake flour
2 tsp. baking powder
¼ tsp. salt
⅓ cup shortening
½ cup sugar

½ cup honey
1 egg
½ cup milk
1 tsp. vanilla extract

Sift dry ingredients together three times. Cream shortening, add sugar gradually and cream until light and fluffy. Add honey gradually, beating after each addition. Add ⅓ cup of sifted dry ingredients. Beat well. Add egg and beat thoroughly. Add remainder of dry ingredients alternately with milk, beating after each addition. Add vanilla.

Bake in two 9-inch greased layer pans in moderate oven (375° F.) 20 to 25 minutes, or until cake shrinks from pan. Spread apricot conserve between layers. Cover top with honey-sweetened whipped cream or fluffy frosting.

Serves 8.

. . . HONEY SPONGE CAKE . . .

1 cup cake flour	¼ tsp. salt
½ cup sugar	½ tsp. vanilla
5 egg yolks	¾ tsp. cream of tartar
½ cup strained honey	2 tbs. boiling water
	5 egg whites

Sift and measure flour and sugar. Beat egg yolks until thick and lemon colored. Add sugar and beat well; add honey and combine lightly. Add boiling water a tablespoon at a time. Beat ½ minute, add flavoring and flour and lastly fold in stiffly beaten egg whites with cream of tartar and salt. Pour into a tube pan and bake for 50 minutes in a very moderate oven (300° F.). When baked, invert on cake rack and allow to cool before removing from pan.

. . . SOFT HONEY CAKE, CORN FLAKES TOPPING . . .

2 cups sifted flour	¼ tsp. allspice
¼ tsp. baking soda	½ cup butter or margarine
¼ tsp. salt	1 cup honey
½ tsp. ginger	1 egg
½ cup buttermilk or sour milk	

Sift together flour, soda, salt and spices.

Blend butter and honey; add egg and beat well. Stir in buttermilk. Add sifted dry ingredients and mix well. Pour into greased 9 x 9-inch pan.

Bake in moderate oven (350° F.) about 45 minutes. Cover with Corn Flakes Coconut Topping.

Broil about 3 minutes or until delicately browned.

Yield: 9 servings.

. . . CORN FLAKES COCONUT TOPPING . . .

1 cup Corn Flakes
2 tbs. butter or margarine,
  melted
¼ cup brown sugar

1 tbs. light cream or
  evaporated milk
¼ cup shredded coconut
¼ tsp. vanilla flavoring

Crush Corn Flakes slightly. Combine with butter, sugar, cream, coconut and vanilla; mix well.

Spread over top of Soft Honey Cake, using fork to distribute evenly.

. . . HONEY ALL-BRAN ORANGE CAKE . . .

1 medium orange
½ cup seedless raisins
¼ cup walnut meats
½ cup All-Bran
1 cup sifted flour

½ tsp. baking soda
½ tsp. salt
½ cup honey
¼ cup shortening
1 egg

* * *

¼ cup honey

¼ cup chopped walnut meats

Grind together whole orange, raisins, walnut meats and All-Bran.

Sift together flour, soda and salt; add honey and shortening; beat about 2 minutes.

Add egg and orange mixture; beat about 2 minutes more. Spread in greased 8 x 8-inch pan.

Bake in moderate oven (350° F.) about 40 minutes.

Drizzle honey over warm cake; sprinkle with chopped walnut meats. Serve warm or cold.

Yield: 1 8 x 8-inch cake.

. . . ITALIAN RUM TORTE . . .
Zuppa Inglese

8 egg yolks	1 spongecake (10-12 inches in
3 level tsp. sugar	diameter)
2 tbs. light honey	1 cup sweet rum
8 half eggshells full of marsala	½ pint whipping cream, chilled
(heavy sweet sherry)	2 tbs. sugar
½ cup chopped glazed fruit	

Zabaglione (Marsala Custard):

Break egg yolks into top part of large double boiler. Add sugar and honey. Beat with egg beater until light lemon color and thoroughly blended. Add marsala; beat thoroughly again.

Place boiling water in lower part of large double boiler. Cook egg-yolk mixture about 5 minutes or until it begins to thicken. Make sure water in lower part boils slowly or mixture will curdle. Beat constantly. Do not allow mixture to boil. Remove top part of boiler upon first sign of bubbles. Set aside to cool.

Slice spongecake into three layers. Place one layer on cake plate; pour ½ cup of rum over it. Cover with ½ of Zabaglione. Place second layer of cake over this, alternate with rum and Zabaglione. Place third layer over this. Chill in refrigerator. When ready to serve, pour cream in mixing bowl. Whip; add 2 tablespoons of sugar; whip until stiff. Spread over top and sides of cake just before serving. Sprinkle with chopped glazed fruit.

Serves 12 to 14.

Honey will give custard smooth delicate flavor.

. . . PECAN-HONEY COFFEE CAKE . . .

2 tbs. honey	⅔ cup milk
2 tbs. melted shortening	2 cups biscuit-mix
1 beaten egg	

Blend first four ingredients; add biscuit-mix. Place in 9-inch greased cake pan and top with Honey Pecan Topping. Bake in moderate oven 375° F. 25 minutes. Makes 8 servings.

. . . HONEY PECAN TOPPING . . .

¼ cup butter or margarine softened	¼ cup warmed honey
⅓ cup solidly packed brown sugar	½ cup chopped pecans

Cream butter, brown sugar and honey until light and fluffy. If too thick, add a few drops of warm water. Spread over batter and sprinkle with pecans.

. . . STRAWBERRY CREAM TORTE . . .

Make your favorite crust for a 9-inch pie shell.

1 quart fresh strawberries	3 tbs. cornstarch
⅔ cup honey	2 tbs. water

Mash strawberries, stir in honey and cook in double boiler. Heat to boiling point; boil slowly for 2 minutes.

Dissolve cornstarch in cold water and stir into mixture. Cook 3 minutes longer or until mixture is smooth and thick. Remove pan from hot water and cool, then pour into baked pie shell; chill until set.

For extra treat garnish with unsweetened whipped cream.

. . . ALMOND SNOOKIES . . .

1 cup butter or margarine	2 cups sifted flour
4 tsp. sugar	2 tsp. baking powder
2 tbs. honey	1 cup chopped almonds
1 tsp. vanilla flavor	Confectioners' sugar
⅛ tsp. almond flavor	

100

Cream together butter, sugar and honey. Add flavors. Stir in flour, baking powder and almonds and blend well. If a little too soft to handle add a tablespoon of flour.

Form into small balls about ¾ inch in diameter and place on ungreased cookie sheet about 1 inch apart. Bake in moderate oven (350° F.) 20 minutes, or until delicately browned. Roll in confectioners' sugar while hot. Yields about 4 dozen cookies.

For Walnut or Pecan Snookies—substitute 1 cup coarsely chopped walnuts or pecans.

. . . HONEY OATMEAL COOKIES . . .

½ cup shortening	1 ⅔ cups rolled oats (oatmeal)
1 cup honey	4 tbs. milk
1 egg	1 cup raisins or
1 ½ cups sifted flour	diced candied fruit
3 tsp. baking powder	¼ cup chopped nuts or peanuts
½ tsp. salt	

Cream together shortening, honey and egg.

Sift dry ingredients and add to oatmeal or rolled oats. Mix well. Add dry ingredients, alternately with milk to the shortening mixture. Stir in fruit and nuts. Drop by teaspoonful on greased baking sheet, an inch apart.

Bake in moderate oven (350° F.) for 15 minutes.

Makes about 3 dozen cookies.

. . . HONEY ALL-BRAN SPICE COOKIES . . .

1 ⅓ cups sifted flour	1 tsp. cinnamon
1 tsp. baking powder	½ cup butter or margarine
¼ tsp. baking soda	¾ cup honey
½ tsp. salt	1 egg
⅛ tsp. ground cloves	1 cup All-Bran
1 cup seedless raisins	

Sift together flour, baking power, soda, salt and spices.

Blend butter and honey; add egg and beat well. Stir in sifted

101

dry ingredients, All-Bran and raisins. Drop by teaspoonfuls, about 2½ inches apart onto lightly greased baking sheets.

Bake in moderate oven (350° F.) about 15 minutes.

Yield: 3 dozen cookies, 2¼ inches in diameter.

. . . HONEY DATE BARS . . .

2 eggs	½ cup All-Bran
¾ cup honey	1 cup cut dates
½ cup sifted flour	½ cup chopped nutmeats
1 tsp. baking powder	Confectioners' sugar
¼ tsp. salt	

Beat eggs until thick; beat in honey, a little at a time.

Sift together flour, baking powder and salt; stir in All-Bran, dates and nutmeats. Add to first mixture and beat well. Spread batter ½ inch thick in greased 9 x 9-inch pan.

Bake in moderate oven (375° F.) about 25 minutes.

Cut into bars while warm and sprinkle with confectioners' sugar. If desired, serve as a pudding with whipped cream.

Yield: 18 bars, 3 x 1½ inches.

. . . HONEY GINGER SNAPS . . .

¼ cup shortening	¾ tsp. soda
¼ cup sugar	½ tsp. salt
¾ cup honey	½ tsp. cinnamon
2 tbs. water	¼ tsp. nutmeg
1 ½ cups sifted flour	¼ tsp. ground ginger

Cream shortening and sugar together. Blend in honey combined with water. Sift flour with soda, salt and spices. Blend into creamed mixture. Drop by teaspoonfuls on well-greased cookie sheet, allowing at least 2 inches between cookies. Flatten slightly with bottom of glass dipped in sugar. Bake in hot oven, 450° F., about 5 minutes. Remove at once with broad spatula and cool on wire rack.

Makes about 3 dozen cookies.

. . . MRS. GINSBERG'S HAMANTASCHEN . . .
(Poppy Seed Cookies)

½ cup honey
2 eggs, beaten
¼ cup sugar
1 cup heavy cream
1 tsp. almond flavoring

3 cups flour
3 tsp. baking powder
1 tsp. salt
2 tbs. poppy seeds

Blend honey in eggs; mix in sugar and cream until smooth; add flavoring. Sift flour, baking powder and salt; mix in poppy seeds and mix into egg mixture. If too sticking add a tbs. of flour. Toss on lightly floured board and knead until smooth, about 5 minutes. Wrap in waxed paper and chill for an hour.

Roll ¼ inch thick on lightly floured board and cut into triangles. Bake on greased cookie sheet at 350° F. about 15 minutes or until delicately browned.

These three-cornered cakes are eaten by the Jews at Purim, which celebrates the release of the Jews by Queen Esther from the viciousness of Haman. The Hamantaschen, a three-cornered cake, represents Haman's hat.

Some make the Hamantaschen by stuffing three-cornered dough with fruit. But Mrs. Ginsberg found these to be preferable.

. . . LACY CORNUCOPIAS . . .

½ cup flour
¼ tsp. baking powder
⅛ tsp. soda
¼ cup clover honey

2 tbs. sugar
¼ cup butter or margarine
½ cup shredded coconut
1 tbs. grated orange rind

Sift together first three ingredients, twice.

Combine honey, sugar and butter or margarine in a saucepan; bring to a slow boil; stir occasionally and boil 1 minute. Remove from heat.

103

Add flour mixture, mix; add coconut and orange rind and mix again.

Drop by ½ teaspoonful on greased cookie sheet, about 2 inches apart to allow for spreading.

Bake in moderate oven, 350° F., 8 to 10 minutes.

Remove from pan with a spatula while still warm. Quickly form into a cornucopia or cone. Place cones on rack to cool. Makes about 2 dozen. Delicious eaten as is or filled with whipped cream. They taste better the following day.

For cocktail tidbits substitute ½ cup of shredded sharp cheese, for coconut, and reduce butter to 2 tablespoons.

. . . . CRISP HONEY WAFERS . . .

Keep some in the refrigerator to bake as needed.

2 ½ cups sifted flour	½ cup shortening
1 ½ tsp. baking powder	½ cup brown sugar
⅛ tsp. soda	1 egg, beaten
½ tsp. salt	½ cup honey

Sift together flour, baking powder, soda and salt. Cream together shortening and sugar. Add egg and beat well. Add honey and mix well. Add flour mixture to creamed mixture. Mix well. Form into two rolls. Wrap in waxed paper and chill. When wanted, cut into slices ⅛ inch thick. Have dough very cold when slicing. Bake on greased cookie sheet in moderately hot oven (350° F.) 10 to 12 minutes. Makes 6 dozen wafers.

VARIATIONS:

. . . CHOCOLATE WAFERS . . .

Omit ¼ cup flour. Sift ¼ cup cocoa with the dry ingredients.

. . . LEMON WAFERS . . .

Add 1 tablespoon grated lemon rind and 1 tablespoon juice to the shortening and sugar.

. . . NUT WAFERS . . .

Add ½ cup finely chopped nuts with the flour mixture.

. . . HONEY BUBBLES . . .
(Strufoli)

2 eggs
1 tbs. melted butter
¼ tsp. salt
1 tsp. vanilla
2 cups flour, sifted
Deep fat or oil

½ cup granulated sugar
½ cup honey
1 tbs. chopped candied fruit
1 tbs. colored sprinkles
1 tbs. chopped nut meats

Beat eggs lightly with butter and salt; add vanilla, and sift in enough flour to make a soft manageable dough. Knead on lightly floured board about 5 minutes. Divide dough in two. Wrap in wax paper and set in refrigerator for half hour.

Roll out dough into oblong pieces about ¼ nich thick. Cut into strips ¼ inch wide. Cut each strip into ¼ inch pieces and spread these little pieces on lightly floured board to prevent sticking. Let stand half hour.

Meanwhile heat fat or oil to 350°, or until a piece of bread dropped in the fat turns brown in 1 minute. Toss in a handful of the dough pieces and cook about 1 minute or until brown all around. These pieces look like little bubbles when done. Remove with perforated spoon, drain well and toss on brown paper to drain some more.

After the bubbles are all done, blend sugar and honey in large skillet and cook over low flame until it comes to a boil, then toss in all the bubbles and stir with wooden spoon until they are all well covered. Remove quickly with wooden spoon and place on platter, in a mound. Top with candied fruit, sprinkles and nuts. Serve when cold. These are good even several days later, if covered with waxed paper and left at room temperature.

. . . SESAME BISCUITS . . .
(Biscotti di Regina)

½ cup sugar	1 tbs. vanilla or orange flavor
1 cup softened shortening	5 cups flour, sifted
1 egg	¾ tsp. salt
¾ cup milk, lukewarm	4 tsp. baking powder
3 tbs. honey	¼ lb. sesame seeds

Cream sugar, shortening and egg. Blend milk with honey and stir into egg mixture. Add flavoring.

Combine flour, salt and baking powder in a bowl; gradually stir in creamed mixture. This should be a soft manageable dough. If too sticky, dust lightly with flour and knead until smooth, about 5 minutes. Wrap in waxed paper and set in refrigerator to chill for an hour or so.

Meanwhile, place sesame seeds in fine sieve and wash with cold running water. Drain well and spread on platter.

Break off pieces of dough, the size of a small walnut. Roll each piece between palms of hands, to resemble a finger. Flatten slightly and roll each piece in sesame seeds. Place on lightly greased cookie sheet about ½ inch apart; bake in 400° oven about 10 minutes, or until golden brown. Yields about 5 dozen biscuits. Excellent with wine, coffee or milk. You'll want to eat them by the dozen.

. . . VERA'S FRUIT NEWTONS . . .

1 cup honey	Juice and grated rind of
1 cup shortening	½ lemon
1 cup sugar	6 ½ cups flour
2 eggs	2 tsp. baking powder
1 tsp. salt	1 tsp. soda

Cream honey, shortening and sugar. Add beaten eggs, lemon juice and rind. Add flour which has been sifted three times with baking powder, salt and soda. Roll dough quite thin, cut into strips about 6 inches long and 3 inches wide. Put filling in center of strip, and lap sides over. Bake 15 minutes 400° F. Cool. Cut into 2-inch pieces crosswise.

. . . RAISIN FIG FILLING . . .

2 cups ground raisins	1 cup honey and ¼ cup water
2 cups ground figs	Juice of ½ lemon and ½ orange
½ cup chopped nuts	

Combine fruit and liquids and cook 15 minutes over medium heat, stirring constantly. Add chopped nuts. Cool before using.

. . . FLAKY PIE CRUST . . .

2 cups sifted flour	¾ tsp. salt
1 tsp. baking powder	⅔ cup butter or margarine
½ cup water	

Sift flour, baking powder and salt in a bowl. Cut in shortening, or mix with fingertips until mixture is mealy. Gradually sprinkle over it enough water to hold ingredients together. Pat into a ball. Chill for about 1 hour. Divide into two parts and roll out between waxed paper.

This makes a two crust pie, or two 8-inch shells.

VARIATIONS:

Sesame Seed Crust—add 1 tablespoon sesame seeds to flour mixture, mix well to distribute seeds, then add shortening; water and proceed as for Flaky Pie Crust.

Flavored Crust—add a tablespoon of sherry, rum, vanilla or almond flavor to the water.

For baked shells, line pie plate, flute-edge of pastry, prick bottom with fork, here and there, and bake about 12 minutes at 400° F.

CUSTARDS, PUDDINGS & FROSTINGS

. . . HONEY TAPIOCA . . .

2 eggs, separated
⅓ cup quick-cooking tapioca
¼ tsp. salt
¼ cup honey
4 cups milk
¼ cup sugar
1 tsp. almond extract

In a saucepan blend egg yolks, tapioca, salt and honey, and cook over low heat with milk, stirring frequently, about 10 to 12 minutes, or until mixture is clear. Remove from fire. Cool slightly. Beat egg whites until stiff; add sugar gradually beating with electric beater or egg beater, and fold into tapioca mixture.
When cooler add flavoring and chill.
Makes 6 to 8 portions.
Serve plain, with fruit sauce or cream.

. . . BANANA FROSTING . . .

⅔ cup mashed ripe bananas
(about 2 bananas)
½ tsp lemon juice
3 tbs. mild honey
¼ cup butter or margarine, softened
2½ cups sifted confectioners' sugar

Cream ingredients in the order named, until smooth and of spreading consistency. If too thick add a bit of honey. Some honeys are thinner than others. If too thin to spread add a little more mashed banana.
Makes about 2½ cups frosting; enough to frost and fill 9-inch layer cake; or 15 to 18 cupcakes.

. . . CHOCOLATE MOCHA FROSTING . . .

½ cup sugar
¼ cup butter or margarine
5 tbs. strong hot coffee
4 tbs. honey

¼ tsp. salt
3 squares bitter chocolate, chopped
2 egg yolks, well beaten

Combine all ingredients in the order named except egg yolks. Melt in top part of double boiler and stir until smooth. Remove from fire. Beat with egg beater. Slowly stir in egg yolks and continue beating with beater. Cook slowly over hot water until mixture thickens. Stir constantly. Remove from hot water and place pan in pan of cold water and continue beating until frosting is light and fluffy.

Enough to cover top and sides of 2 eight-inch layer cakes.

. . . EASY CHOCOLATE FROSTING . . .

3 squares bitter chocolate chopped
⅛ tsp. salt

3 tbs. honey
1 tsp. orange flavor
1 tsp. grated orange rind

Melt chocolate over hot water. Add balance of ingredients in the order named. Remove pan from hot water and whip until smooth and creamy, and of spreadable consistency.

Enough for 8-inch square cake.

. . . PLAIN CHOCOLATE FROSTING . . .

½ cup buckwheat honey
2 tbs. sugar
¼ tsp. cream of tartar

1 egg white
½ tsp. vanilla
¼ cup cocoa

Mix all ingredients except cocoa in top of double boiler. Place over boiling water and beat with egg beater until mixture forms peaks, about 4 minutes. Remove from heat and fold in cocoa. Makes enough for filling and top of 9-inch layer cake.

For white frosting omit cocoa, and add another white of a small egg.

. . . YUMMY CHOCOLATE FROSTING . . .

½ cup sugar
¼ cup butter
¼ cup light cream
¼ cup honey

¼ tsp. salt
3 squares unsweetened
    chocolate, cut in small pieces
2 egg yolks, well beaten

Combine sugar, butter, cream, honey, salt, and chocolate in top of double boiler. Place over boiling water. When chocolate is melted beat with rotary beater until blended. Pour small amount of mixture over egg yolks, stirring vigorously. Return to double boiler and cook 2 minutes longer, or until mixture thickens slightly, stirring constantly. Remove from hot water, place in pan of ice water or cracked ice, and beat until of right consistency to spread.

Enough for two 8-inch layer cakes.

. . . FLUFFY HONEY FROSTING . . .

2 egg whites   ½ cup honey
                  Dash of salt

Beat egg white with salt until stiff and stands in peaks. Pour honey in fine stream over egg white, beating constantly until frosting holds its shape (about 4 minutes).

Enough for top and sides of a small 2-layer cake.

. . . SEVEN MINUTE HONEY FROSTING . . .

¼ cup honey
¾ cup sugar
1 egg white

3 tbs. lemon juice
Dash of salt
½ tsp. grated lemon peel

Combine honey, sugar, egg white, lemon juice and salt in top part of double boiler. Place over boiling water and beat with whirl-type beater about 7 minutes, or until frosting thickens and holds its shape when dropped from beater. Remove from heat and add grated lemon peel. Continue beating until thick enough to spread.

Yield: Frosting for two (8-inch) layers.

. . . CRUSTED HONEY ALMOND CREAM . . .

1 tbs. unflavored gelatin	¼ tsp. vanilla flavoring
1 ¾ cups milk	⅛ tsp. almond flavoring
2 eggs, separated	1 ½ cups Rice Krispies
⅛ tsp. salt	¼ cup chopped nutmeats
½ cup honey	1 tbs. melted butter or margarine

Soften gelatin in ¼ cup of the milk.

Heat remaining milk over boiling water.

Beat egg yolks with salt and ¼ cup of the honey. Combine with milk and cook until mixture coats a metal spoon. Remove from heat; stir in softened gelatin. Chill until mixture begins to set.

Beat egg whites until stiff but not dry; fold in remaining honey, a tablespoonful at a time. Fold into custard mixture together with flavorings. Pour into 8 x 8-inch pan rinsed with cold water.

Crush Rice Krispies slightly; mix with nutmeats and melted butter. Brown in oven. Sprinkle over pudding. Chill until firm. Cut into squares to serve.

Yield: 9 servings.

. . . APRICOT HONEY BREAD PUDDING . . .

½ cup butter, melted	¼ tsp. mace, or nutmeg
½ tsp. cinnamon	⅓ cup honey
¼ tsp. salt	1 tbs. lemon juice
1 ½ cups, drained, diced canned apricots	4 cups bread cubes (½ inch) toasted

In small saucepan, over low heat, melt the butter. Stir in the cinnamon, salt, mace, honey and lemon juice. In a bowl, combine butter mixture with the diced apricots and toasted bread cubes. Turn into a greased baking dish (1¼ quarts). Bake in moderate oven, 350° F., for 30 minutes. Serve warm with sweet or sour cream, whipped or plain.

Serves 4 to 6.

. . . TOASTED ALMOND CUSTARD . . .

5 egg yolks	½ tsp. almond flavoring
2 cups scalded milk,	⅛ tsp. salt
slightly cooled	8 marshmallows, cut in half
¼ cup honey	2 tbs. chopped toasted almonds

In a fireproof bowl beat egg yolks slightly. Gradually stir in milk; add honey, flavoring and salt and mix until well blended. Place bowl in pan of boiling water almost to level of custard. Bake in moderate oven 325° F. for 45 minutes or until a silver knife comes out clean when inserted in center. Remove dish from water and place marshmallows cut-side down over surface of custard. Sprinkle with chopped almonds. Cool and chill.

Makes 4-5 servings.

. . . HAZELNUT PUDDING . . .
(Budino di Nocciole)

3 cups milk	1 tbs. cherry liqueur or
3 eggs, beaten	cherry flavoring
2 tbs. cornstarch	4 lady fingers
⅓ cup orange or lemon	¼ lb. toasted shelled hazelnuts,
blossom honey	chopped

Dissolve cornstarch in ¼ cup of the milk. Add balance of milk, eggs and honey. Pour in a saucepan and beat with egg beater until fluffy. Cook over low flame about 10 minutes, or until it boils; boil 1 minute or until mixture coats spoon; stir constantly. Remove from fire and add flavoring.

Crumble lady fingers and mix with chopped nut. Fold into

112

pudding. Spoon into sherbets or custard cups; chill in refrigerator. Serves 8.

Packaged vanilla pudding may be used, but you must add one tablespoon honey and 1 teaspoon of cornstarch while dissolving. Proceed with lady fingers and nuts as above.

. . . HONEY FIG PUDDING . . .

¼ cup butter or margarine	½ cup All-Bran
⅔ cup honey	1 cup sifted flour
1 egg	½ tsp. baking soda
½ cup milk	½ tsp. salt
1 cup finely cut dried figs	

Blend butter and honey; add egg and beat well. Stir in milk and All-Bran.

Sift together flour, soda and salt; add to All-Bran mixture together with figs, mixing well. Fill greased 1-quart mold two-thirds full. Cover tightly.

Steam about two hours. Slice and serve hot with hard sauce or other suitable pudding sauce.

Yield: 6-8 servings.

NOTE: If figs are very dry, cover with boiling water and let stand about 10 minutes. Drain thoroughly before cutting into pieces.

. . . ORANGE CUSTARD . . .

2 tbs. butter	1 tbs. lemon juice
¼ cup sugar	1 tsp. grated orange rind
2 eggs, separated	¼ cup honey
2 tbs. flour	1 cup milk
¼ cup orange juice	

Cream butter and blend in sugar. Add egg yolks and beat until fluffy. Add flour and beat until smooth. Stir in orange, lemon juice, rind, honey and milk. Fold in stiffly beaten egg whites; pour into buttered 5-cup casserole or into 4 custard cups. Set in shallow pan of hot water and bake in slow oven, 300° F.,

1 hour for casserole, or 45 minutes for the custard cups, or until a silver knife inserted in the center comes out clean.

Serve either warm or cold.

Four servings.

. . . MARISSA'S APPLE PUDDING . . .

5 large green apples
2 tbs. white clover honey or a mild blend
½ tsp. vanilla or almond flavor

2 cups coarsely ground zweibach crumbs
½ cup melted butter or shortening
½ tsp. allspice

Whipped cream

Peel, core and slice apples rather thickly. Place in saucepan; add enough cold water to nearly cover the apples and simmer until almost cooked, about 10 minutes. Remove from fire; stir in honey and flavor.

Butter a medium sized baking dish. Place in it a layer of crumbs and top with apples; alternate layers of crumbs and apples and top with crumbs. Use enough crumbs to make a fairly solid dish. Pour over all the melted butter or shortening. Dust with allspice.

Bake for 30 minutes at 375° F. or until firm. Turn out on serving dish and top with whipped cream or chilled whipped evaporated milk.

Makes 4 to 6 servings.

. . . RICE SUPREME . . .

2 cups heavy cream
¾ cup confectioners' sugar
1 tbs. sherry or rum

1½ cup boiled rice
2 tbs. gelatin
1 tbs. orange blossom honey

½ cup water

Combine cream, sugar and sherry; mix well and add rice. Stir.

Soften gelatin in water 3 minutes; stir in honey. Stir over

114

hot water until dissolved. Combine with rice mixture; stir well and turn into a quart mold.

Chill in refrigerator until set.

Serve with honey-almond sauce or any fruit sauce.

For a festive occasion, pour over each portion some cherry liqueur.

FROZEN DESSERTS

. . . APRICOT PARFAIT . . .

2 cups dried apricots	1 (14 ½ oz.) can evaporated
4 cups water	milk
½ cup granulated sugar	2 tsp. plain gelatin
½ cup honey	3 tbs. cold water
	1 tsp. vanilla extract

Cover apricots with 4 cups water and cook about 10 minutes. Add sugar and honey and cook 5 minutes longer. Remove from heat and sieve; beat. Scald milk. Soften gelatin in cold water and dissolve in hot milk. Chill until milk thickens slightly; beat with rotary beater until light and fluffy. Gradually beat apricot mixture into thickened milk. Blend in flavoring. Spoon into serving dishes or custard cups and chill in refrigerator 1½ to 2 hours, or until firm.

Serves 8 to 10.

. . . AVOCADO SHERBET . . .

2 large ripe avocados	1 tbs. sugar
1 tsp. lime or lemon juice	1 tbs. honey

Cut avocado in half lengthwise, remove large seed and peel. Mash into a pulp with a fork or potato masher; add lime or lemon juice, sugar and honey. Blend with blender or whip until creamy.

Spoon into 3 or 4 sherbet cups and chill until very cold. Serve with sprig of fresh mint and a maraschino cherry.

. . . BANANA SHERBET . . .

2 cups mashed bananas	¼ cup light honey
(4-5 bananas)	½ tsp. salt
2 tbs. lemon or lime juice	1 egg white, beaten stiff
¼ cup sugar	2 cups milk

Mix banana and juice thoroughly. Combine sugar, honey and salt and blend into bananas. Fold in stiff egg white, and slowly stir in the milk.

Turn into refrigerator trays to freeze. Stir occasionally to keep from getting icy. When firm and smooth serve.

Serves 6 to 8.

. . . GRAPEFRUIT SHERBET . . .

1 tbs. gelatin	1 cup mild honey
2 tbs. cold water	2 cups grapefruit juice
1 cup boiling water	Juice of 1 small lemon
Maraschino Cherries	

Soften gelatine in cold water. Add boiling water and honey. Stir until dissolved. Cool and add juices. Freeze in refrigerator trays. Stir occasionally to prevent from getting too hard. Top with cherries.

Serves 6 to 8.

... FROZEN CREAM TOPPING ...

½ cup evaporated milk,
  chilled

1 tbs. honey
1 tsp. grated orange rind

Whip evaporated milk; fold in honey; beat until smooth. Pour into refrigerator tray; freeze until firm but not icy, about 45 minutes. Fold orange rind into cream. Serve on stewed dried fruits or cooked fruits, or plain cake.
Makes 4 portions.

... HONEY ICE CREAM ...

2 cups milk
¾ cup honey

¼ teaspoon salt
2 eggs
1 cup heavy cream

Scald 2 cups whole milk in double boiler; add honey and salt. Beat eggs. Pour scalded milk slowly into the egg mixture and beat until well blended; cook for three or four minutes. Cool. Beat cream and fold into custard mixture. Freeze in refrigerator trays. Stir once or twice while freezing. Serve with honey almond sauce or a tart fruit sauce.

... HONEY GRAHAM CRACKER ICE CREAM ...

1 ½ cups fine Honey Graham
  cracker crumbs
1 cup top milk
1 ½ tsp. vanilla

¼ tsp. salt
1 ½ cups whipping cream
½ cup honey

Combine all ingredients except cream. Whip cream, and add to other ingredients. Pour into refrigerator trays. When partially set, beat with rotary beater. Return to refrigerator trays and let freeze until firm. 8 servings.

117

. . . LEMON ICE CREAM . . .

2 eggs	2 cups cream, whipped
½ cup sugar	1 tsp. grated lemon rind
½ cup honey	3 tbs. lemon juice

Set control of your refrigerator for fastest freezing.

Beat eggs until thick and lemon-colored. Gradually beat in sugar and honey. Beat until light and fluffy. Add lemon rind and juice. Beat again and fold in whipped cream until lightly blended.

Pour into two freezing trays. Freeze until firm, but see that it does not harden and get icy.

Then, pour into chilled bowl; break up mixture with a wooden spoon. Mix quickly for a minute; and return trays to refrigerator to keep cold. Beat mixture vigorously with a beater, or electric beater, for 2 more minutes or until it becomes light and creamy. Spoon quickly into the chilled freezing trays. Moisten bottom of trays to make contact quickly and return at once to freezing compartment to finish freezing. When frozen, reset control to normal temperature to mellow ice cream until time to serve.

Serves 6.

. . . HONEY MARSHMALLOW ICE CREAM . . .

15 marshmallows	2 eggs, separated
1 ½ cups milk	Dash of salt
3 tbs. honey	1 cup heavy cream, whipped

Slice marshmallows and mix with milk, honey and egg yolks. Cook over hot water in double boiler until mixture coats spoon. Cool. Store in refrigerator about 4 hours but do not freeze.

Then whip egg whites with salt until stiff; fold into mixture. Pour into freezing trays (half full). When mixture gets mushy fold in the whipped cream and let it harden at coldest temperature.

118

FRUIT ICE CREAMS:

Add ¼ cup crushed pineapple; or sliced peaches; or strawberries; or raspberries to mixture just before you fold in whipped
cream, and proceed as for Honey Marshmallow ice cream.

. . . JELLIED HONEY DESSERT . . .

1 3-oz. package lemon	¼ cup honey
flavored gelatin	¼ tsp. salt
¾ cup boiling water	2 tbs. lemon juice

1 cup whipping cream

*   *   *

1 ½ cups Rice Krispies	1 tablespoon butter or
¼ cup chopped nutmeats	margarine, melted

Dissolve gelatin in boiling water. Add honey, salt and lemon
juice; mix well. Chill until mixture begins to set.

Whip cream until stiff; fold into gelatin mixture. Pour into
10 x 6-inch pan.

Crush Rice Krispies into fine crumbs; mix with melted butter
and nutmeats. Sprinkle over pudding. Chill until firm. Cut into
squares to serve.

Yield: 6 servings.

. . . MARRON SOUFFLÉ . . .

1 ¼ lbs. chestnuts	1 egg white, beaten stiff
¼ cup sugar	1 cup whipping cream
⅓ cup honey	2 tbs. confectioners' sugar

Wash chestnuts; cover with water; boil in covered pot 30
minutes or until very soft. Drain; cool. Remove shells and skins.
Mash with fork or potato masher, until consistency of mashed
potatoes. Add ¼ cup sugar and honey, beat; fold in egg white,
turn into chilled tube or ring mold (1½ quart) and chill until set.

Whip cream with confectioners' sugar until stiff.

Before serving, unmold on cold platter and fill hollow with

whipped cream. If no mold is available, spoon mixture into custard cups and top with whipped cream.

Serves 6.

. . . HONEY BUTTER ELYSIAN . . .

1 cup clover honey
½ cup sweet butter or
margarine

¼ cup grated orange rind

Have ingredients at room temperature. Blend honey and butter in a bowl over hot water. Mix in the orange rind. Remove bowl from hot water and beat until mixture is fluffy. Store in covered jar in refrigerator.

This is excellent on toast, hot biscuits, waffles, pancakes and even plain fresh bread.

. . . HONEY BANANA MOLD . . .

2 tbs. gelatin
¼ cup cold water
1 ½ cups milk
½ cup mild honey

3 bananas, mashed well
1 tbs. lemon juice
1 cup whipped cream

Soak gelatine in cold water until soft. Heat milk, remove from fire and stir in gelatine. Add honey, mashed bananas and lemon juice. Mix well and cook. When mixture begins to thicken fold in whipped cream. Spoon into quart mold and chill thoroughly.

Serves 4.

. . . PERSIMMON WHIP . . .

1 cup persimmon pulp
½ cup honey
3 tbs. lemon juice

5 egg whites, beaten stiff
¼ tsp. salt

Heat pulp and honey in saucepan over low heat until well

120

blended. Remove from fire; add lemon juice. Beat and fold in the stiff egg whites.

Spoon into buttered baking dish and set in pan of hot water; bake in slow oven, 300° F. for 1 hour, or until set but not dry.

Serve hot or cold, plain or with whipped cream or chilled sweetened whipped evaporated milk.

Serves 3-4.

. . . PRUNE ALMOND WHIP . . .

12 dried prunes, pitted	2 cups milk, scalded
12 blanched almonds, shredded or coarsely chopped	2 eggs, separated
	2 tbs. sugar
	2 tbs. honey

Cut prunes into small pieces. Combine with shredded almonds and place in well buttered or greased baking dish. Allow milk to cool. Beat egg yolks with sugar and honey until creamy and smooth. Beat into milk.

Whip egg whites until stiff and fold into egg mixture, carefully. Pour in baking dish over prunes and almonds.

Bake in 350° F. oven until custard has set (about 30 to 40 minutes).

Serve cool or cold with whipped cream or milk. Serves 4.

. . . ROYALE CREME . . .
(Ricotta Condita)

1 lb. ricotta (Italian cottage cheese)	3 tbs. rum or more to taste
¼ cup milk	2 tbs. fine grind or pulverized black coffee (demitasse coffee)
2 tbs. mild honey	

Combine ricotta, milk, honey and sieve to blend and refine. This should be of custard consistency. Chill. Before serving mix in rum. Spoon into sherbert or custard cups and dust with fine grind or pulverized coffee.

This makes a delightfully simple dessert, and your friends will love it.

. . . HONEY MOUSSE . . .

½ cup crushed pineapple (drained)
½ cup orange blossom honey (warmed)
½ cup nut meats, chopped
½ cup diced candied fruit

1 tsp. vanilla extract
2 egg whites
¼ cup powdered sugar
1 cup heavy cream

Mix pineapple, honey, nut meats, candied fruit and vanilla. Cool. Beat egg whites until stiff and add sugar. Beat cream until stiff. Fold all ingredients together and freeze either in paper mousse cups or in freezing trays.
Serves 4 to 6.

. . . TROPICAL MOUSSE . . .

1 cup sieved avocado pulp
3 tbs. honey
¼ tsp. salt

1 tsp. lemon extract
2 egg whites, beaten stiff
1 cup whipped cream

Combine sieved avocado pulp with honey, salt, and extract, and blend thoroughly. Add to stiffly beaten egg whites in small portions, beating well after each addition. Fold into whipped cream, blending thoroughly but lightly. Place in bowl in freezing unit approximately 2½ hours or until set. Serves 4 to 6.

FRUIT, CONFECTIONS, CONSERVES

. . . APPLES SUPREME . . .

6 large eating apples
⅓ cup seedless raisins chopped
1 tbs. honey
Dash Nutmeg

1 tbs. lemon juice
1 tbs. chopped nuts
2 oz. cream cheese blended with 1 tbs. honey

122

Wash and core apples. Leave a bit of the core at bottom of each apple so filling will not go through.

Combine raisins, honey, lemon juice and nuts. Fill each apple. Brush with a little honey. Place about ½ inch of water in a baking pan and put apples in. Bake at 400° F. until tender. Or cook covered on top of stove.

When done dust each apple with a dash of nutmeg and top with cheese honey mixture.

Serves 6.

. . . FRUIT MELBA . . .

Cut one small melon, honeydew, cantaloupe, persian or any desired melon, with a melon ball cutter. Do the same with 2 large apples, 2 large pears, 1 avocado, and any other fruit you like. Add a few strawberries or cherries. Mix balls with a syrup of two parts honey to one part lemon juice and chill. This combination makes a wonderful fruit cup; everybody loves it. Serve with a sprig of mint.

. . . CRANBERRY ALMOND MOLDS . . .

1 cup cranberries	1 package lemon-flavored
¼ large orange (including rind)	gelatin
¼ cup granulated sugar	1 ½ cups hot water
¼ cup honey	Roasted blanched almonds
	Salad greens

Rinse and drain cranberries. Put through food chopper with orange, using medium knife. Stir in sugar and honey and let stand 1 hour or more. Dissolve gelatin in hot water and cool until slightly thickened. Arrange whole almonds in bottom of 6 small oiled molds; pour thin layer of gelatin around them and allow gelatin to set. Stir cranberry mixture into remaining gelatin and spoon into molds. Chill until firm. Unmold on salad greens and serve as relish or salad. Serve with Turkey or Game.

Serves 6.

. . . BROILED GRAPEFRUIT . .

4 grapefruit halves   4 tbs. sherry
4 tsp. honey   4 maraschino cherries

Loosen pulp from peel with a sharp knife. Remove seeds. Cut out tough fibrous center with scissors.

Combine honey and sherry and pour over fruit. Place on cold broiler rack set about 4 inches below burner. Broil at medium heat, 375° F., for about 15 minutes or until slightly brown.

Serve hot with a cherry in the center.

. . . GRAPEFRUIT MERINGUE . . .

For special occasions, top each half with a honey-sugar meringue instead of the sherry. Use 1 egg-white for 2 halves.

Bake in oven at 400° F. till meringue is delicately browned (about 10 minutes).

MERINGUE:

Beat 2 egg whites until foamy, beat in a pinch of cream of tartar (1/16 tsp.) and ¼ cup honey; beat vigorously until mixture holds up in peaks.

. . . WATERMELON MARASCHINO . . .

3 cups diced watermelon pulp   4 tbs. maraschino liqueur
½ cup orange blossom honey   Fresh mint leaves
                                Chopped almonds

Combine lightly the pulp and honey. Chill for 2 hours. Then transfer to 4 sherbet glasses and pour one tablespoon of the liqueur over each sherbet. Dust with chopped almonds and garnish with mint leaves. Chill for another half hour.

Very refreshing and different.

Juice of maraschino cherries may be substituted or any flavored liqueur.

Serves 4.

124

. . . APRICOTS MARSALA . . .

12 large ripe apricots   2 tbs. honey
          ⅓ cup Marsala or dry sherry

Select firm ripe fruit. Wash and dry gently. Cut in half; remove stones. Place in dish. Combine honey and sherry and pour over fruit. Turn fruit so it will be soaked well. Cover dish and chill in refrigerator.

Serve 3 halves per portion; pour over each portion some of the liquid, and add a bit of sherry if necessary.

Serves 4.

. . . CHILDREN'S PARTY RING . . .

½ cup honey   6 cups wheat flakes or rice
¼ cup sugar   krispies (5 cups)
½ tsp. salt   ⅓ cup chopped nuts
½ tbs. butter or margarine

Combine honey, sugar and salt, and cook 10 minutes, in a saucepan, over medium heat. Add butter and mix. Add flakes and nuts, stirring lightly to coat flakes. Remove from fire. Press into well greased ring mold. When cool unmold and fill center with ice cream, fruit or fruit-flavored gelatin.

Yields 6 to 8 portions.

. . . PARTY SQUARES . . .

Take small squares of yellow or chocolate, plain cake; spread top and sides with honey butter; roll in chopped nuts or chopped shredded coconut. Place on cookie sheet. Toast in 350° F. oven for 10 minutes or until delicately browned.

Serve with vanilla ice cream topped with honey and chopped nuts for extra special treat.

. . . HONEY RICE KRISPIES CHOCOLATE SQUARES . . .

2 cups (12 oz.) semi-sweet chocolate pieces

⅔ cup honey
5 cups Rice Krispies

Melt chocolate over hot but not boiling water; stir in honey. Remove from heat. Add Rice Krispies, mixing thoroughly.
Press into buttered 15 x 10-inch pan. Let stand until hardened. Cut into squares or bars.
Yield: 35 squares, about 2 x 2 inches.

. . . HONEY CARAMELS . . .

¾ cup sugar
¼ cup honey
¼ cup brown sugar
2 tbs. butter

¼ cup milk
½ cup cream
½ tsp. vanilla

Combine all ingredients except vanilla in a saucepan. Cook to 253° F. Stir frequently to prevent scorching. Remove from flame. Add vanilla and pour into buttered 8-inch pan. When cold, cut with sharp knife and wrap each piece in wax paper.

. . . HONEY CHEWS . . .

½ cup butter or margarine
1 cup honey

½ cup chopped dates or prunes
1 cup chopped nuts

Cook butter and honey over low flame about 50 minutes or until mixture reaches 266° F. on a candy thermometer. Stir frequently. Remove from fire. Add dates and nuts. Mix well and pour into well-greased 8-inch square pan. Let cool. Cut into squares. Wrap in wax paper.
If you do not have a candy thermometer, it might be worth while purchasing one for a few cents. It comes in handy for deep frying and many other uses, and insures the success of your recipes.

126

. . . CRYSTAL CINNAMON CARAMELS . . .

1 ½ cups sugar	2 tbs. water
½ cup honey	1 tsp. cinnamon
	1 tbs. lemon juice

Blend sugar, honey and water in a heavy saucepan. Cook over low heat about 10 minutes or until mixture boils. Boil slowly 5 minutes, stirring constantly to make smooth mixture. Boil 5 minutes without stirring, or until a teaspoonful dropped in cold water forms hard ball. Remove from heat. Blend in cinnamon and lemon juice. With a damp cloth, wipe off any crystals that may form on sides of pan. Pour mixture into well greased pan about 1½ inches deep by 8 inches square. When it cools a little mark into squares. When candy hardens remove carefully from pan and break into squares.

When we were children, grandmother gave us these for sore throats.

. . . DIVINITY DROPS . . .

2 cups sugar	⅓ cup water
⅓ cup honey	2 egg whites
	½ cup chopped nut meats

In saucepan, boil sugar, honey, and water until syrup spins a thread (278° F.). Pour syrup over well-beaten egg whites, slowly, beating continuously. Just before mixture starts to set, add chopped nut meats. When mixture crystallizes, drop by tablespoonful on waxed paper.

Variation: Candied fruit may be added.

. . . HONEY-GLAZED BRAZIL NUTS . . .
(Noce al Miele)

1 cup honey	½ cup sugar
	1 lb. Brazil nutmeats

127

Blend honey and sugar in heavy saucepan and let it come to a slow boil. Boil slowly about 15 minutes or until a small amount dropped in cold water forms a firm ball. Remove from heat. Drop nutmeats in honey mixture and roll or coat every nut. Remove with candy fork; place on waxed paper or platter and set aside in cool dry place until glaze hardens.

Almonds, filberts, walnuts or pecans may be glazed this way.

. . . MOCHA ROLL . . .

1 cup brown sugar, firmly packed	1 tsp. orange flavor
¼ cup light honey	1 cup or (6 oz. pkg.) Chocolate bits
¼ cup evaporated milk	1 tbs. instant coffee

1 cup nuts, coarsely chopped

Combine first three ingredients and bring to a boil. Boil 2 minutes, stirring constantly. Remove from heat.

Add flavor, chocolate bits and coffee and beat until smooth. Mix in the nuts until well distributed.

Shape on waxed paper in two 12-inch rolls. Roll up and chill. Cut in half-inch slices.

Makes about 1¼ pounds candy.

. . . PEANUT HONEY CANDY . . .

½ cup butter or margarine	½ cup boiling water
1 cup honey	¼ tsp. glycerin
1 cup sugar	⅛ tsp. soda

⅓ cup toasted peanuts

Combine all ingredients except peanuts in a glass or enamel saucepan and bring to a slow boil; boil slowly 12 minutes. Remove from fire. Cool slightly and stir in peanuts. Pour into a well greased shallow 6-inch square pan. Mark into squares and cut through when cold and set.

The children will love it.

. . . POPCORN WALNUT BALLS . . .

1 cup honey	½ cup walnut meats coarsely
3 cups popped corn	broken up

Bring honey to a slow boil in a skillet; boil slowly 2 minutes; stir in popped corn and walnuts; when cool form into small balls. Place on waxed paper until ready to eat.

Substitute peanuts for walnuts if you wish.

. . . TORRONE . . .
(Nugat Cremona)

3 egg whites	½ lb. shelled toasted hazelnuts
1 cup sugar	¾ lb. shelled almonds, toasted
1 cup honey	¼ lb. pistachio nutmeats or
1 tsp. vanilla	pine nuts
¼ tsp. salt	

Beat egg whites until stiff.

Cook sugar and honey slowly in a saucepan, stirring constantly and bring to a slow boil. At first sign of bubble remove from fire. Add vanilla, salt. Stir with wooden spoon. Fold into egg whites. Add nuts in the order named and stir after each addition. Cook over low flame for 10 minutes, stirring.

Pour mixture quickly into a thickly buttered pan 10 inches square by 1½ inches deep. Spread evenly and pack down with wooden spoon. Cool 5 minutes. Cut through with sharp-pointed knife into 1 or 2 inch squares. When cold and hard, turn pan over on platter, board, or porcelain or marble table top; if torrone is not cut all the way, break off as cut; separate pieces; wrap each piece in waxed paper and store in airtight container until used. Yields about 2 pounds of crisp nugat and keeps for weeks.

This is a Christmas and Easter Italian specialty. It derives its name from the famous torrione (tower) of the Cathedral of Cremona, where it was originally made by the monks.

. . . TURKISH DELIGHT . . .

5 tbs gelatin
½ cup cold water
¼ cup hot water
1 cup sugar
1 cup honey
¼ tsp. salt
½ cup orange juice

3 tbs. lemon juice
Green vegetable coloring and
   ¼ tsp. mint flavoring or red
   coloring and 1 tsp. almond
   flavoring
1 cup finely chopped nuts

Soften the gelatin in the cold water for 5 minutes. Bring the hot water, sugar, and honey to the boiling point. Add salt and gelatin, stir until the gelatin has dissolved, and simmer for 20 minutes. Remove from fire, when cool, add the orange and lemon juice, coloring, and flavoring. Stir in the nuts and allow the mixture to stand until it begins to thicken. Stir again before pouring into a wet baking pan; have the layer of paste about an inch thick. Let stand overnight in a cool place. Dip a sharp knife into boiling water, cut the candy into cubes, and roll in powdered sugar.

Add coloring by the drop until you get desired color.

If stronger mint flavor is desired add a little more flavoring.

. . . APRICOT CONSERVE . . .

1 ½ cups dried apricots
   tightly packed

2 cups honey
1 cup coarsely ground nut meats

Rinse apricots in hot water, drain and put through food chopper, using a fine knife.

Bring honey slowly to the boiling point, remove from heat; add apricots and nuts and blend well.

Pour into sterilized glasses; seal with paraffin.

Let stand for 3 or 4 days before using.

130

. . . BLACKBERRY CONSERVE . . .

3 cups fresh blackberries	2 tbs. chopped fresh mint leaves
2 cups honey	½ cup walnuts broken into small pieces

Wash and drain berries. Bring honey to a slow boil; remove from heat; stir in mint leaves and nuts and fold in berries. Proceed as for Apricot Conserve.

. . . PEACH CONSERVE . . .

Follow same directions and quantities as for Apricot Conserve. Use dried peaches.

Honey is known to be an extraordinary preservative, and for persons who cannot take sugars, honeyed preserves are a great aid in satisfying that craving for sweets.

. . . FRUIT BALLS . . .

¼ cup dried prunes	½ cup dates
¼ cup dried apricots	¼ cup raisins
¼ cup dried figs	⅓ cup honey
½ cup chopped nutmeats	

Wash prunes and apricots and soak in boiling water 5 minutes. Run all the fruit and ½ of the chopped nuts through a food chopper, fine knife. Add honey. Mix. With buttered hands shape into small balls. Roll in rest of chopped nuts.

Any dried fruit may be used.

. . . ORANGE BALLS . . .
(Pallottole d'Aranci)

½ lb. fresh orange peels	3 tbs. honey
4 tbs. sugar	1 tsp. vanilla
¼ lb. chopped mixed nuts	

Use about six large California navel oranges. Peel thickly with sharp knife. Soak peels in cold water for 24 hours. Drain. Weigh peels. Place in saucepan; cover with cold water; bring to a boil. Cook about 10 minutes or until soft; drain.

Chop orange peels fine or put through food chopper; mix with sugar and honey. Cook slowly over low flame about 10 minutes or until a small quantity dropped into cold water forms a soft ball. Add vanilla; blend thoroughly. Remove from fire; cool; shape into small balls about size of small walnut. If too soft add a tablespoon or 2 of chopped nuts. Roll in sugar; dip in finely chopped nuts. Something different!

THIRST QUENCHERS

. . . HONEYED BEVERAGES . . .

Honey dilutes easier in warm liquids than cold. When making drinks with honey, always dilute the honey in a little of the liquid that has been warmed slightly. Then add to cold liquids.

. . . HONEY-LEMONADE . . .

1 tbs. fresh lemon juice	1 tbs. warm water
1 tbs. honey	1 cup water or soda water

Combine lemon juice, with honey diluted in warm water. Mix well. Stir into water or soda. Chill, or add 1 or 2 ice cubes, before drinking.

To Honey-Lemonade add 6 tbs. orange juice, 1 tbs. pineapple juice and a few fresh crushed strawberries. Mix well and pour into tall glasses half full of cracked ice .

. . . FRUIT PUNCH . . .

½ cup blossom honey
Juice of 1 large orange
1 cup crushed pineapple

1 quart unsweetened grape juice
½ cup crushed bing cherries
(fresh or canned)
Fresh mint leaves

Heat honey and orange juice until well blended. Remove from fire. In punch bowl combine all of the ingredients except mint. Mix well; pour in tall glasses filled with cracked ice. Top with mint leaves.

Punch can be served in punch cups from the bowl. Place ice cubes in bowl and pour punch over ice.

. . . HOLLYWOOD HONEY PUNCH . . .

1 ½ qts. water
Honey to sweeten
Juice 6 large lemons
Juice 6 large oranges

1 cup tamarind juice
1 cup guava or currant juice
1 cup shredded or
crushed pineapple
Fresh mint leaves

Heat 1 cup of the water to lukewarm and blend with 1 cup of honey. Add to balance of water and stir thoroughly. Add juices and pineapple. Chill. When ready to serve pour over cracked ice and garnish with mint leaves.

Add more honey if necessary.

Yield: About 3 quarts.

133

. . . AMBROSIA . . .

1 cup orange juice	¼ tsp. salt
½ cup grapefruit juice	1 quart milk
1 tbs. lemon juice or lime juice	⅓ cup honey or more to taste

Combine fruit juices and salt. Warm 1 cup of milk and blend in the honey; add this to cold milk and stir well.

Add milk mixture gradually to the fruit juices. Beat with egg beater, electric mixer or blender until thoroughly blended and smooth.

Chill and serve. Excellent as a one-glass lunch treat, for those who are having light lunches.

. . . SPICED MILK . . .

¼ tsp. cinnamon	2 cups evaporated milk diluted
⅛ tsp. grated mace	with 2 cups water
3 tbs. honey	

Blend the spices with the honey until smooth. Warm the diluted milk and beat into the honey mixture.

Serve warm or chilled.

. . . COFFEE BANANA FLOAT . . .

1 ripe banana	½ cup heavy cream
1 cup strong, cold coffee	1 cup cold milk
1 tsp. very mild honey or	1 tsp. vanilla
avocado honey	3 scoops coffee ice cream

Mash banana with fork or in an electric blender. Add coffee, honey and cream. Beat with rotary beater or in blender until thoroughly mixed. Add milk and vanilla. Mix well. Pour into three tall glasses. Add 1 scoop of coffee ice cream to each glass.

. . . NEW YEAR COFFEE NOG . . .

2 egg yolks
⅓ cup instant coffee
Dash salt
1 tbs. vanilla
4 tbs. mild honey

¾ cup brandy or sherry
2 cups milk
2 egg whites, beaten stiff
1 cup heavy cream, whipped

Combine and beat until thick first 4 ingredients. Combine 2 tablespoons of honey with brandy and milk and beat into egg yolk mixture. Chill.

Beat egg whites with balance of honey until very stiff and satiny and fold into egg yolk mixture. Fold in whipped cream.

Chill again if desired, and serve in cups or glasses.

Serves about 12.

. . . ICED CHOCOLATE . . .

1 cup hot milk
2 tsp. cocoa

2 tbs. honey
Pinch of salt

Place all ingredients in a bowl and beat with egg beater until thoroughly blended.

Serve hot or pour in tall glasses filled with cracked ice. Top with meringue or whipped cream if desired.

. . . HONEY EGG-NOG . . .

2 eggs
2 tbs. honey, or more if desired

1 quart of milk
Cinnamon or nutmeg

Beat eggs with honey until frothy; gradually beat in milk. Place in refrigerator to chill. Serve with dash of cinnamon when desired.

For an added treat, add a teaspoon of rum or sherry to each serving.

135

. . . HONEYED COCOA . . .

⅓ cup cocoa
⅛ tsp. salt
2 cups water

2 cups fresh or evaporated milk
¼ cup honey

Mix cocoa and salt. Add water and bring to a boil. Stir frequently, and boil 2 or 3 minutes. Add evaporated milk and honey. Heat thoroughly and serve hot.

If you use fresh milk omit water and use 4 cups of fresh milk. Four to 6 servings.

. . . GRAPEFRUIT OR ORANGE NOG . . .

1 tall can of evaporated
milk (1 ⅔ cups)
1 cup water, tepid

¼ cup honey
1 No. 2 can grapefruit or
orange juice (2 ¼ cups)

Pour milk into a bowl and beat, until bubbly. Blend honey in water and mix into milk. Slowly add juice to milk mixture and beat vigorously while pouring to avoid curdling. Chill and drink. 4-6 servings.

. . . HONEY MINT SYRUP . . .

1 tsp. mint extract or
10 fresh mint leaves
(washed and dried)

¼ cup honey
2 tbs. lemon juice

Crush mint leaves until very soft, if you use fresh mint.

Combine mint or mint extract with honey and juice and blend with a spoon until smooth and creamy.

Keep in jar, tightly covered, in refrigerator and use as needed. Excellent on vanilla ice cream or in drinks.

. . . LEMON FIZZ . . .

Make honey lemonade as above, and to each glass add ½ glass of gingerale and ½ teaspoon of honey mint syrup.

Serve chilled.

136

. . . HONEY SPICED TEA . . .

4 level tbs. tea
1 tsp. whole cloves
1 cup strained orange juice

½ cup lemon juice
⅔ cup honey, or more to taste
8 cups freshly boiled water

Pour 5 cups boiling water over the tea and cloves in a china or enamel bowl; steep 5 minutes, strain; add juices, honey and remaining 3 cups of hot water. Stir until honey is thoroughly dissolved. Serve hot.

Makes 8 to 10 servings.

. . . TEA COLLINS . . .

Pour honey spiced tea in tall glasses over cracked ice. Garnish with maraschino cherry and fresh mint leaves.

. . . HONEY TANG . . .

1 quart sweet cider
¼ cup honey
2 inch stick of cinnamon

1 tsp. allspice
⅛ tsp. salt
6 whole cloves

Place all ingredients in a glass or enamel pot. Bring slowly to a boil. Boil 5 minutes. Remove from fire and allow to stand several hours. Then strain, heat and serve.

This makes an excellent winter drink.

. . . HONEY TOMATO JUICE COCKTAIL . . .

2 cups tomato juice
4 tbs. lemon juice or lime juice

2 tsp. honey
¼ tsp. salt

Combine and beat vigorously. Chill and serve.

. . . VITALITY COCKTAIL . . .

1 cup orange juice
1 tbs. lemon juice or lime juice

2 tbs. honey
1 egg yolk

Warm orange juice and lemon juice slightly and beat in the honey, egg yolk. Beat vigorously.

Chill and serve. This is a wonderfully nourishing and excellent one-glass meal.

. . . BLACKBERRY LIQUEUR . . .
(Liquore di More)

2 quarts ripe blackberries	1 pint acquavit or alcohol
⅛ tsp. cinnamon	½ cup sugar
1 clove	1 cup orange blossom honey

Wash berries; mash in bowl with fork; strain through cheesecloth. This should yield about 2 cups juice.

Place juice in quart jar; add cinnamon, clove and alcohol. Blend well. Seal jar and set aside 4 weeks. Then blend in sugar and honey until sugar and honey are dissolved. Filter through paper filter or fine linen cloth; pour into sterilized bottles and cork tightly; set aside 3 days and filter again. Bottle and cork tightly.

If you use acquavit, eliminate sugar.

Delightful, deep amethyst colored, after dinner liqueur. Honey makes it smooth.

. . . COLUMELLA . . .
(Honey-wine)

1 pint tart wine	½ cup orange blossom honey

Blend a cup of wine with the honey. Add to balance of wine. Store in a fifth bottle, tightly corked, and set aside for 4 weeks.

This makes a mellow delicate wine.

It can be served as a liqueur or a dessert wine.

. . . ANDERSON'S HONEY WINE . . .

1 large box grapes	3⅓ gallons cold water
3⅓ gallons of honey (mild flavored)	10 gallon wooden keg

138

Large box of grapes for wine-making usually weighs about 42 to 45 pounds.

Press grapes in wine press, or mash well. Set aside in keg 4 or 5 days or until grapes stop bubbling. To prevent dust from getting into grapes cover loosely with cheese cloth. Then strain well. This should give you about 4 gallons of grape juice. Pour in keg, add the honey and water and stir until well blended. Cover keg and set aside in cool dry place for about 6 weeks or until wine settles and clears.

CHAPTER VI

Bringing up Baby

DOCTORS and nutritionists the world over, have written papers on the beneficial effects of honey in infant feeding. Honey has long been recognized as a satisfactory supplement to the infant's diet.

It is admitted that breast milk from a normal mother is the best food for babies. However, this natural food is often deficient in quality and quantity for the baby as he develops. Modified cow's milk must then be given to replace or supplement the mother's milk. Various sweetening agents have been used to make the cow's milk conform more to the requirements of the baby. Glucose (dextrose) and dextri-maltose have been the sugars most commonly used for this purpose. In recent years, experiments made by leading clinics and pediatricians at the Truby King Hospitals and Baby Health Centres in Australia and New Zealand, as well as in other parts of the world, have shown that honey is superior for modifying cow's milk. Honey is the ideal sweetener for babies. Bacteria, the cause of diseases in human beings, cannot live in honey. Furthermore, it is palatable, easily digested, alkaline and slightly laxative. We have learned, too, that honey contains vitamins and calcium in small quantities, among other minerals, influencing the retention of calcium so beneficial to young infants.

Ask your doctor to recommend a formula which includes honey for your baby. It will help immeasurably in his development.

141

Here are some formulae which have been helpful at my home; perhaps they will help your baby too.

Please make sure you buy the purest, mildest honey available for this purpose.

FOR UPSET STOMACH

Four oz. of barley water, combined with ½ tsp. of honey, given lukewarm, should help your baby. If it does not, call your doctor.

FOR BLOATED STOMACH

One tsp. of mild honey in fresh or evaporated milk, lukewarm.

Or, 2 oz. of parsley water with ¼ tsp. of honey. *Parsley Water:* Combine 4 oz. of water with 4 sprigs of fresh washed parsley. Boil 5 minutes. Strain and cool.

Warm milk with enough honey to sweeten, poured over baby's cereals and strained baby foods makes them more palatable and nourishing.

CHAPTER VII

A Word to the Wise

GENERAL DIRECTIONS:

1. Read your recipes carefully.
2. Assemble all your ingredients and utensils before starting.
3. Turn on your oven and set thermometer at desired temperature.
4. Grease all pans that require greasing or product will be sticky.
5. Measure ingredients carefully with standard measuring cups and spoons.
6. Sift flour once before measuring. Pile lightly in cup (do not pack or shake cup). Level off with straight edge knife.
7. Cornmeal, whole wheat, bran or rye flours should be stirred, not sifted, to lighten, then measure as other flours.
8. Unless otherwise stated, use mild flavored honeys in liquid form. Select your special honey flavor and keep it on hand.
9. Honey, eggs and shortening should be at room temperature for easier mixing.
10. Keep honey in tightly covered jar in a dry place at room temperature.
11. When cake pans are taken out of oven, cake should not be removed from the pan until cake cools slightly and becomes firmer. Cake is too soft and hot for handling when it first comes out of the oven. It should be removed from the pan before it reaches room temperature or has a chance to sweat.

143

12. If honey becomes crystalized, just put jar in a bowl of hot water and keep it there until honey becomes clear and liquid again (about 10 minutes).
13. Pick a cool, dry day to make candies and frostings when using honey or part honey, because humidity keeps candy and frostings soft and sticky.
14. Oven temperatures should be kept low when baking with honey, otherwise baked goods brown too quickly.
15. After you choose your favorite flavor, it is wise to buy honey in 5-lb. containers, because it is more economical.
16. Honey retains moisture, and for that reason baked goods stay fresh longer. So that you can do your baking in advance, especially around the holidays, without fear of spoiling or getting stale.
17. Measuring honey: Honey drains slowly from measuring cup because it is thick. If fat is measured first and honey measured in the same cup, the coating of fat will enable the honey to pour more readily from the cup. A rubber scraper or spatula will help remove the last drops of honey left in measuring cup or spoon.

ADAPTING YOUR FAVORITE RECIPES TO HONEY

BEST RESULTS ARE OBTAINED IF:

Part sugar and part honey is used.

All pure honey is used in pies, dark cookies, spice and fruit cakes, breads and toppings.

Half honey and half sugar is used in chocolate cakes, pound cakes and light cookies.

One-third honey and two-thirds sugar is used in white and yellow layer cakes.

One-fourth honey and three-fourths sugar on icings, candies and frostings.

The above proportions will adapt your favorite all-sugar recipe to honey, if you wish to do so.

144

Clover honey for light colored cakes, cookies and candies.
Orange or Lemon blossom honeys for salad dressings and fruit drinks.
Buckwheat, Sage and Wild Thyme honey for spicy baking.
Tupelo or any mild honey for toppings, icings and frostings because it does not crystalize easily.
However, there are hundreds of honey flavors, and selecting any brand or flavor is like selecting any brand of beverage or food. It is a matter of taste and preference. I suggest you try various types and choose your favorite.

FOR EASY POURING:

Combine in a small jar ½ cup of honey with two tablespoons of warm water. Mix until well blended. Use this to pour over hot cereals, fruits, pancakes, waffles and berries. Delicious! For added glamour add a teaspoonful of grated orange or lemon rind to the honey.

USING THE RIGHT BAKING PAN

Using the right pan is just as important for good results as the use of the right ingredients.
Use shiny tin or aluminum pans for baking cakes, cookies, pies, breads and biscuits if you want a tender, delicate-brown-colored crust on these products. It has been found that shiny tin or aluminum (light colored metals) reflect the heat away from the pan and do not darken your baked products before they are done.
On the other hand, if you use a glass baking dish or use a darkened pan, you will get a dark brown, heavy crust on your baking. If you prefer the dark brown crusts on your cakes, pies, bread and biscuits, then use old darkened pans. It is a matter of taste and choice. I, personally, prefer the more delicately browned baked goods.

However, if you have only dark tins and you want a delicate brown color for your cakes and pies, then it is well to reduce the temperature about 20 degrees from what the recipe calls for. Dark pans attract or absorb the heat and so the cakes and pies darken faster.

It might be well the next time you bake to experiment a little along these lines. I have found the right baking pan to be very important.

CLARIFIED BUTTER

Cooking and frying with butter is sometimes a very discouraging chore. Butter turns dark and sometimes black when using high heat. Certainly it is not very appealing unless we want "Beurre noir" for some special dish.

Here is an easy way to cook with butter without worrying about its turning black.

Place one pound of butter, sweet or salted, in a saucepan. Heat it very slowly until it is melted. Continue cooking until dark specks and foam appear on top and a residue forms at bottom of pan. This residue and the dark specks and foam are the casein in milk. Skim off the foam and dark specks. Cool slightly. Then strain melted butter through a linen cloth, into a clean bowl or jar. When cold, cover and put it in the refrigerator. It will last indefinitely. Use for cooking only.

Chapter VIII

Taste Teasers

SANDWICH FILLINGS:

1. Mix 2 dried apricots, chopped with 2 tbs. cottage cheese and 1 tsp. of honey, and chopped nuts.
2. Cream together: 1 tbs. honey, 1 tsp. butter, 1 tbs. chopped nuts and ¼ tsp. grated orange rind.
3. Cream together: 1 tbs. honey, 3 tbs. cottage cheese or 2 tbs. cream cheese with 1 tsp. chopped chives or olives.
4. Cream together: 1 tbs. honey, 1 tbs. peanut butter, 2 large dried prunes, chopped.
5. Cream together: 2 tbs. chopped ham or tongue, 1 tsp. honey, top with tomato slices, and lettuce.
6. Cream together: 1 tbs. anchovy paste, blended with 1 tsp. honey; top with tomato and lettuce.
7. Cream together: 2 tbs. chopped chicken, or any cooked meat chopped, 1 tsp. honey, 1 tsp. finely chopped celery or watercress.
8. Cream together: 1 tbs. crumbled roquefort cheese, 1 tsp. honey and 1 tbs. fig preserve.
9. Cream together: 2 tbs. grated American cheese, 1 tsp. honey, 3 black olives chopped.
10. Mix together: 2 slices of crisp bacon crumbled with 1 tsp. honey, 1 tsp. chopped sweet basil leaves.

Whole wheat, rye bread, bran bread or gluten bread sandwiches with the above fillings and lettuce are delicious. For weight control do not use butter on the bread.

Bread or toast spread with honey butter alone, is a treat for you and your children. It makes a good after school snack.

. . . WATERCRESS TEA SANDWICHES . . .

¼ cup of Honey Butter
1 tbs. lemon juice
¼ tsp. salt

2 tbs. chopped watercress
1 tbs. chopped nut meats
Fresh Bread

Sprigs of watercress

Cream honey butter and lemon juice. Stir in chopped watercress and nuts. Spread on thin slices of fresh bread (crust trimmed off) and roll up. Place a sprig of watercress in each end.

Serve immediately. Or if you wish to serve later on, cover plate with sandwiches with a damp towel and keep in refrigerator.

. . . OPEN FACE TOASTIES . . .

½ cup honey butter
¼ cup chopped ham or
crisp bacon

1 ½ tbs. chili sauce
Sweet pickles or Gerkins
Fresh Bread

Toast 1 side of thin sliced white bread, from which crust is removed. Cut into 4 squares. Combine all ingredients and mix thoroughly, except pickles. Spread on untoasted side of bread; toast lightly under broiler. Garnish each square with a thin strip of pickle; serve hot.

. . . DATE & NUT BREAD-PEANUT BUTTER SANDWICHES . . .

12 thin slices Date & Nut Bread
¼ cup of peanut butter

1 tbs. honey
1 tsp. milk

Blend peanut butter, honey and milk and spread on 6 of the slices; cover with other slices.

. . . CELERY-ENDIVE . . .

12 thin slices of Date & Nut Bread

4 endive leaves, chopped

2 tbs. honey mayonnaise or honey french dressing

⅔ cup chopped celery

Pinch of salt

Blend mayonnaise with chopped endive and celery, add salt. Spread on 6 slices of bread, cover with remaining slices.

. . . EGG-PIMENTO . . .

2 tbs. Honey French Dressing

2 tbs. chopped pimentoes

3 hard-cooked eggs, chopped

1 tsp. chopped olives

6 slices fresh bread

Mix all ingredients and spread on 3 slices of thin bread. Top with lettuce leaf and cover with remaining slices.

. . . PARTY LOAF . . .

¼ cup chopped cooked chicken

1 cup shredded lettuce or endive

4 tbs. butter or margarine

2 small tomatoes sliced thin

Salt and pepper to taste

9 oz. cream cheese

1½ cups grated American Cheese or Old English Cheese

Bunch of Radishes

Watercress

⅔ cup of Honey French Dressing

1 loaf fresh unsliced bread

Trim crust from loaf of bread and cut in 4 slices lengthwise.

Blend chopped chicken, butter and salt and pepper, and spread on slice of bread; blend cheese with 1/3 cup of the dressing and spread on another slice of bread and place over chicken mixture. Place slice of bread over this and spread with shredded lettuce or endive combined with balance of dressing, top with tomato slices and season with salt and pepper. Cover with fourth slice of bread. Press top slice slightly so as to make loaf firm.

Blend cream cheese with 6 additional tablespoons of dressing, and spread on top and sides of loaf. Place on platter. Cover with waxed paper and chill in refrigerator for about 5 hours.

Before serving cut down into slices about 1 inch thick. Garnish with radishes that have been washed and peeled to resemble rose, and watercress.

Serves 6.

. . . SKYSCRAPER SANDWICH . . .

Day-old bread   Tomatoes
Olive Pimento Cheese Spread   Cream Cheese
Honey French Dressing   Milk

Slice bread ¼ inch thick; cut into rounds with a biscuit or doughnut cutter, about 2½ inches in diameter. Cover one round with cheese spread and place on it another round spread with dressing. Top with a slice of peeled tomato and cover with a third round of bread spread with dressing.

Soften a stick of cream cheese with a little milk and blend well. Frost top and sides of each sandwich. Garnish with parsley or watercress.

Serve 2 to each person with shredded carrot and chicory salad with French dressing.

. . . CHEESE DIP . . .

½ lb. cream cheese   2 tbs. butter or margarine
¼ lb. Gorgonzola or Roquefort   2 tbs. honey
cheese   ½ tsp. Worcestershire Sauce
½ lb. pimento cheese   Dash of Paprika

Melt cheese in top part of double boiler, stirring constantly to blend well. Add butter, honey, sauce and paprika. Remove from fire. Beat until fluffy. If too thick add a tablespoon or two of warm milk and beat. Dip should be consistency of thin custard.

Pour in bowl; set in center of large round plate and surround with potato chips, crackers, apple slices, boiled shrimp,

150

tiny meat or fish balls, cocktail frankfurters, and other cocktail tidbits.

Your guests will have fun dipping these tidbits.

. . . CHEDDAR CHEESE WAFERS . . .

¼ cup butter or margarine
¼ tsp. tabasco
1 tsp. honey

3 oz. cheddar cheese (softened)
⅔ cup sifted flour or more if needed

Paprika

Cream butter; add tabasco and honey and cream well. Blend in cheese and enough flour to form a medium manageable dough. Form into roll about 1 inch in diameter. Wrap in waxed paper and chill several hours, or overnight. Slice 1/8 inch thick. Bake on ungreased cookie sheet in 350° F. oven, 12 to 15 minutes. Sprinkle with paprika. Serve with cocktails. Makes about 3 dozen wafers.

. . . HONEY-CHEESE DROPS . . .

6 oz. cream cheese or cottage cheese
2 tbs. honey

½ cup graham cracker crumbs or chopped nuts

Cream the cheese with the honey until smooth. Chill for ½ hour. Then form into small balls between palms of hands and roll in crumbs or chopped nuts. Chill thoroughly before serving. These may be prepared the day before a cocktail party.

. . . PARTY CHEESE TIDBIT . . .

6 oz. Roquefort cheese
10 oz. Cheddar cheese spread
¾ lb. cream cheese
2 tbs. grated onion

1 tsp. Worcestershire sauce
2 tsp. mild honey
1 cup coarsely ground walnuts or any other nuts
½ cup finely chopped parsley

Let cheeses soften at room temperature. Combine softened

151

cheeses, onion, Worcestershire sauce and honey; blend. Stir in
½ cup ground walnuts and ¼ cup chopped parsley; mix well.
Shape mixture into large ball. Wrap in wax paper and chill
overnight.

About 1 hour before serving, roll ball in remaining walnuts
thoroughly mixed with parsley; place on decorative platter,
and surround with crackers and clusters of grapes, apples and
pears.

Excellent on crackers with cocktails or after dinner. Good
with fruit too.

BREAKFAST—EYE OPENERS

Leading nutritionists and medical authorities recommend a
good breakfast of fruit, cereal, milk, bread and butter and eggs.
This, they say, sets one up for the tasks of the day ahead and
makes life pleasanter and easier all around. A good breakfast
also prevents that midmorning hunger and tired feeling. The
quantity of the food eaten should be adapted to the size and
activity of the individual, but the kinds of food needed are
the same for everyone.

Of course, there are those who prefer to eat meat and potatoes and even pies and fish for breakfast, but that is a matter
of taste and preference. The effect is probably the same, inas-
much as these are substantial foods.

However, I am inclined to agree that the foods suggested by
the nutritionists and medical authorities, as good breakfast
combinations, are preferable for most people. After a stretch of
10 or 12 hours the heavier foods might cause the stomach to
rebel. Be that as it may, each to his own taste.

Here are a few suggestions that might make your breakfast
more pleasant and digestible:

ORANGE JUICE:

Some persons are allergic to orange juice before breakfast,
because they say it gives them a sour stomach and leaves a

152

sour taste. If that is the case with you, the acid will be neutralized if you add a half teaspoon of honey to your orange juice. This is true also of unsweetened grape juice and grapefruit juice.

GRAPEFRUIT:

A little honey drizzled over your grapefruit is delightful. It's good on cantaloup or berries as well.

CEREALS:

Milk and honey poured over hot or cold cereals gives energy and is delicious. This is especially good for children.

TOAST, FRENCH TOAST, MUFFINS, BISCUITS, WAFFLES, GRITS, PANCAKES:

A mixture of equal parts honey with butter or margarine and grated orange rind, spread on these, is a taste thrill that you'll remember all day long. Or just use plain honey if you like.

HONEY-BUTTER:

Is very soothing to the lining of your stomach and is especially desired for persons who are not allowed to eat sugars for one reason or another.

Combine equal parts of honey with butter; blend well and store in covered jar in refrigerator.

Coffee, tea and cocoa, sanka and postum, sweetened with honey are delicious. Milk with honey given to children gives them added energy and a sweet disposition.

ANOTHER BREAKFAST TREAT:

Fried hominy with honey. Crisp bacon and peach halves filled with melted butter or margarine and honey, baked for 15 minutes.

MENU SUGGESTIONS

On a Sunday morning try feeding your family with the following:

> Fresh Pineapple Slices with honey
> Scrambled eggs with bacon strips
> Orange Honey Muffins
> Honeyed Cocoa or Milk, Coffee

On Blue Monday, this one might help:
> Honeyed Fruit Juice or Grapefruit
> Cooked Cereal with Honeyed Milk
> Bran Coffee Cake made with honey
> Beverage same as for Sunday

On Tuesday:
> Baked Apples with honey
> Orange Waffles with Honey Butter
> Broiled Sausages
> Same beverages

On Wednesday:
> Stewed Prunes and Apricots
> Uncooked Cereal with Honey Milk
> French Toast with honey
> Beverages as above

On Thursday Try This:
> Broiled Grapefruit with honey
> Fried Cornmeal Mush with honey
> Broiled Bacon or Canadian Ham
> Cocoa, Coffee or Milk

On Friday:
> Fresh Berries or Sliced Bananas
> Ready-to-eat Cereal with honey
> Plain Omelet
> Raisin Muffiins with Honey Butter
> Coffee, Cocoa, Tea or Milk

154

On Saturday:
Stewed Fruit
Griddle Cakes with Honey Orange Butter
or Hot Biscuits with Honey Butter
Coffee, Cocoa, Tea or Milk
Any of these ought to start the day right.

STANDARD WEIGHTS AND MEASURES

	APPROXIMATELY
2 cups fat, cottage cheese or sugar (granulated), rice	1 pound
3-1/3 cups confectioners' sugar	1 pound
2¼ cups brown sugar, firmly packed	1 pound
4 cups white flour	1 pound
3½ cups graham flour	1 pound
16 ounces, solid	1 pound
2½ cups raisins	1 pound
3½ cups walnuts, pecans, chopped	1 pound
2 cups liquid	1 pint
4 cups liquid	1 quart
16 tablespoons liquid	1 cup
4 tablespoons flour	1 ounce
3 teaspoons	1 tablespoon
2 level tablespoons butter or shortening	1 ounce
8 ounces liquid	1 cup
3 large eggs	2/3 cup
8 to 10 egg whites	1 cup
2 large eggs	½ cup
4 to 5 lemons (large)	1 cup juice
Dash	1/16th teaspoon

. . . HONEY . . .

1 cup equals	12 ounces
1¼ cups equal	1 pound
1½ tablespoons equal	1 ounce

155

tsp.—teaspoon	pt.—pint
tbs.—tablespoon	qt.—quart
lb.—pound	gal.—gallon
oz.—ounce	hr.—hour
mod.—moderate	min.—minute

A FEW SUBSTITUTES

1 teaspoon baking powder,	equals 1/3 teaspoon soda plus ½ teaspoon cream of tartar
1 cup honey	equals ¾ cup granulated sugar plus ¼ cup liquid
1 cup butter	equals ⅞ cup lard
1 square unsweetened chocolate	equals 3 to 4 tablespoons cocoa plus 1 teaspoon shortening
1 tablespoon cornstarch for thickening	equals 2 tablespoons flour
1 cup milk	equals ½ cup evaporated milk and ½ cup water
1 cup soured milk	equals 1 cup sweet milk plus 4 teaspoons lemon juice or cider vinegar
1 cup whipping cream	equals 1 cup of very cold evaporated milk whipped in chilled bowl
1 cup canned tomatoes	equals about 1-1/3 cups cut fresh tomatoes, firmly packed, simmered 10 minutes

CHAPTER IX

Honey in the Holy Bible

THE use of honey as a staff of life is stressed in the Old and the New Testaments. Honey represented the height of purity and virtue, not only in connection with its food value but also in its therapeutic values.

In the hope that you will find them interesting I mention a few excerpts taken from the Douay and King James Versions of the Holy Bible:

Apoc. 10:9. And He said to me: Take the book and eat it up, and it will make thy belly bitter, but in thy mouth it will be sweet as honey.

Canticles (Solomon) 4:11. Thy lips, my spouse, are as a dropping honeycomb; honey and milk are under thy tongue.

Canticles 5:1. ° ° ° I have eaten the honeycomb with my honey. ° ° °

Deuteronomy 8:7-8. For the Lord thy God bringeth thee unto a good land, a land of brooks and water, of fountains that spring out of valleys and hills; a land of wheat, barley, vines, fig trees and pomegranates; a land of olives, oil and honey.

Ecclesiasticus (Wisdom Praises Herself) 24:27. For my spirit is sweet above honey and my inheritance above honey and the honeycomb.

Ecclesiasticus (The exercises of wise men) 39:31. The principal things necessary for the life of men, are water, fire and iron, salt, milk, bread and honey and the cluster of grape and oil and clothing.

Ecclesiasticus 49:1,2. The memory of Josias is like the composition of a sweet smell made by the arts of a perfumer. His remembrance shall be sweet as honey in every mouth, and as music at a banquet of wine.

Ezekiel 16:13. * * * Thus saith the Lord God unto Jerusalem: * * * Thus wast thou adorned with gold and silver; and thy raiment was of fine linen and silk and embroidered work; thou didst eat fine flour and honey and oil; and thou wast exceedingly beautiful and was advanced to be queen.

Ezekiel 20:2,6. Then came the word of the Lord unto me saying, * * * In the day that I lifted up mine hand unto them, to bring them out of the land of Egypt, into a land that I had provided for them, flowing with milk and honey, which excels all lands.

Ezekiel 27:2,17. Now, thou son of man, take up a lamentation for Tyrus; * * * Judah, and the land of Israel, they were thy merchants with the best corn; they set forth and traded in thy market, honey and oil and balm and rosin.

Isiah 7:15,14,22. Therefore the Lord Himself shall give you a sign. Behold, a virgin shall conceive and bear a son, and shall call his name Emmanuel. Butter and honey shall he eat that he may know to refuse the evil and choose the good.

Judges 14:7,8,9. After a time he returned to take her, and he turned aside to see the carcass of the lion; and behold, there was a swarm of bees, and honeycomb in the mouth of the lion. And he took thereof with his hands and went on eating, and came to his father and mother, and he gave them, and they did eat; but he told them not that he had taken the honey out of the carcass of the lion.

Jeremiahs 41:8. But then ten men were found among them that said to Ismahel: Kill us not for we have stores in the field, of wheat and barley and oil and honey.

Job 20:17 (Downfall of the wicked). Let him not see the streams of the river; the brooks of honey and of butter.

3. Kings 14:3 (Son of Jeraboam fell sick). Take also these

10 loaves and cracknels and a pot of honey and go to him, for he will tell thee what shall become of this child.

1. Kings 14:25,26,27,29,43 (Attack of the Philistines). All the common people came into a forest in which there was honey upon the ground. * * * And when the people came into the forest, behold the honey dropped, but no man put his hand to his mouth; * * * But Jonathan had not heard when his father adjured the people, and he put forth the end of the rod, which he had in his hand, and dipped it in the honeycomb, and he carried his hand to his mouth, and his eyes were enlightened.

* * * And Jonathan said: My father hath troubled the land; you have seen yourselves that my eyes are enlightened because I tasted a little of this honey. And Saul said to Jonathan: Tell me what thou has done and Jonathan said to him: I did but taste a little honey with the end of the rod, which was in my hand, and behold I must die.

Luke 24:33,34,36,39,41-43. And they * * * returned to Jerusalem and found the eleven gathered together, and them that were with them, saying: The Lord is risen indeed and hath appeared to Simon. And as they thus spoke, Jesus himself stood in the midst of them, and saith unto them, Peace be unto you. But they were terrified and frightened and supposed that they had seen a spirit. And he said unto them Why are ye troubled and why do thoughts arise in your hearts? Behold my hands and my feet, that it is I myself; handle me and see; for a spirit hath not flesh and bones as ye see me to have. And while they yet believed not and wondered for joy, he said unto them: have you here anything to eat? And they gave him a piece of broiled fish and a honeycomb. And he did eat before them.

Mathew 3:4. But St. John himself had a garment of camel's hair and a leather girdle around him and his food was locusts and wild honey.

Numbers 16:12,14. * * * And Moses sent to call Dathan and Abiram, the sons of Eliah. But they said, we will not come. Thou hast brought us indeed into a land that floweth with milk

159

and honey, and hast given us possession of field and vineyards; wilt thou also pull out our eyes? No, we will not come.

Psalm 18:10,11. The fear of the Lord is Holy, enduring forever and ever; the judgments of the Lord are true and righteous altogether. More to be desired are they than gold, yea, than much fine gold and many precious stones; sweeter also than honey and the honeycomb.

Psalm 80:16,17. The enemies of the Lord have lied unto him. He fed them with the finest wheat and with honey out of the rock.

Psalm 118:103. How sweet are thy words to my palate. Yea, sweeter than honey to my mouth.

Proverbs 16:24. Pleasant words are as honeycomb, sweet to the soul and health to the bones.

Proverbs 24:13,14. My son, eat thou honey, because it is good, and the honeycomb most sweet to thy throat. And wisdom be unto your soul when thou has found it * * * .

Proverbs 25:16. Hast thou found honey? Eat so much as is sufficient for thee lest thou be glutted therewith.

Proverbs 27:7. The soul that is full loatheth the honeycomb; but to the hungry soul every bitter thing is sweet.

Glossary

Ambergris:	A waxy substance used in perfumery and cosmetics. Purchased at drug stores.
Bake:	To cook by dry heat in oven.
Batter:	Thin mixture of flour, liquids and eggs.
Blanch: (nuts)	To place in boiling water for a few minutes; remove and quickly plunge into cold water; remove skins by slipping nuts between fingers.
Baste:	To moisten with liquid while roasting, prevents dryness.
Blend:	To combine slowly until mixture is even and smooth.
Boil:	To allow to boil, bubble.
Boiling point:	Temperature reached when mixture or water maintains a full bubbling motion on the surface.
Broil:	To cook under direct heat.
En Brochette:	Cooked on a skewer.
Coat Spoon:	When mixture forms thin film on spoon.
Honeycomb:	Lattice-like waxy section taken from the beehives. It has honey in the waxen cells.
Cool:	After pan has been taken from fire, set in cool place. Cool is temperature between warm and cold.
Clarified Butter:	Butter that is cooked slowly to melting point and heated until brown specks or sediment forms at top and bottom of pan; then strained through linen cloth to clarify. Clarified butter never burns like ordinary butter.

161

Crystalized Honey:	Ground honey crystals that have granulated naturally.
Whipped Honey:	Granulated honey that is whipped to a creamy consistency.
Cream:	To make soft, smooth and creamy by mixing; blending.
Dissolve:	To combine a dry and liquid substance and blend.
Dot:	To place a small piece over the surface.
Drizzle Honey:	Place jar of honey in pan with warm water for about 10 minutes. Then let it drip in thin threads over fruit, cereal, pancakes, waffles. If a little honey is diluted with lukewarm water it flows freely, or it can be poured through a syrup jar with a spout; or just spooned out of jar. Equal parts of honey and lukewarm water, blended, make a free-flowing syrup.
Dough:	A stiff mixture of flour, liquid, etc., which is easily handled, rolled or kneaded.
Fat:	Butter, margarine, lard, oleo, bacon fat.
Fusilli:	Short curly spaghetti.
Grind:	To reduce to small pieces or powder.
Knead:	To roll and press firmly with the hands.
Marsala:	A creamy sweet sherry (Italian).
Mash:	To soften by pressing or squeezing.
Melt:	To heat solids until they turn liquid.
Mix:	To combine ingredients until evenly distributed.
Paste:	A fine, smooth mixture; also a dough.
Pasta:	A dough or macaroni product.
Peel:	To remove outer covering.
Ricotta:	Italian creamy-pot cheese.
Sauté:	To cook in fat or oil slowly, until soft but not brown or crisp.
Scald:	Temperature just below boiling point.
Shred:	To cut or tear into thin strips.
Sift:	To put through a fine sieve.

162

Soften:	To mash until smooth and creamy.
Stir:	To blend ingredients in circular motion.
Steam:	To cook, covered, over boiling water.
Toast Nuts:	Place unshelled nuts on a cookie sheet or shallow baking pan and roast in 375° F. oven, for 15 or 20 minutes. Then cool and shell. (Shake pan occasionally to make sure shells don't burn while roasting.)
Unmold:	To remove from a container or mold.
Whip:	To put air into a mixture by beating with a brisk rotary motion or a blender.

Index

168